FARSCAPE™

THE ILLUSTRATED COMPANION

FARSCAPE: THE ILLUSTRATED COMPANION

1 84023 178 5

Published by
Titan Books
A division of
Titan Publishing Group Ltd
144 Southwark St
London
SE1 0UP

First edition September 2000
2 4 6 8 10 9 7 5 3 1

ACKNOWLEDGEMENTS
The authors would like to thank the following for their help in turning round this book so easily: all of those we interviewed for so graciously giving up their time, often at the end of gruelling days on set; Brian Henson, Pete Coogan, Karen Harper and Brian Deputy at The Jim Henson Company; Fiona Searson at DDA, Australia, and Sandy Stevens on the *Farscape* set, for facilitating the interviews; Rod Edgar and Jacquie Bance for research back-up; Ruth Thomas for co-ordination above and beyond the call of duty; Adam Newell, David Barraclough and Oz Browne at Titan; and especially Rockne S. O'Bannon and David Kemper for always being available for questions and discussion despite all the many other calls on their time.

DEDICATION
For my parents, for a love of writing, reading and not persuading me to give up watching science fiction!
— Paul Simpson

To Liz, for encouraging my lifelong fascination with the fantastique, and Zahida, for enjoying *Farscape* enough to watch it over, and over, and over...
— David Hughes

What did you think of this book? We love to hear from our readers. Please e-mail us at: readerfeedback@titanemail.com or write to Reader Feedback at the address above.

Titan Books are available from all good bookshops or direct from our mail order service. For a free catalogue or to order, phone 01858 433169 with your credit card details, e-mail asmltd@btinternet.com or write to Titan Books Mail Order, Bowden House, 36 Northampton Road, Market Harborough, Leics, LE16 9HE. Please quote reference FS/IC.

A CIP catalogue record for this title is available from the British Library.

Printed and bound in Great Britain by MPG, Bodmin, Cornwall.

FARSCAPE™

THE ILLUSTRATED COMPANION

Paul Simpson and David Hughes

Series created by Rockne S. O'Bannon

TITAN BOOKS

CONTENTS

FOREWORD

"**M**ommy, I want to be Gene Roddenberry when I grow up."

Okay, I didn't actually say that when I was a kid watching the original *Star Trek*. But the sentiment must have sunk in on some subliminal level. To a ten-year-old anxious to see what amazing alien life form Kirk and Spock were going to encounter that week, the letters c-r-e-a-t-e-d-b-y-g-e-n-e-r-o-d-d-e-n-b-e-r-r-y flying past at the beginning of each episode were no more than a curious blur and minor distraction.

I mean, who really reads all those names with arcane titles at the beginning of their favourite TV shows anyway?

Cut to: half a lifetime later, when Brian Henson approached me with the remarkable opportunity to create a television series utilising every facet of his incredible imagination factory, The Jim Henson Company. My chance to "be Gene Roddenberry when I grew up" had arrived.

The result is the series that is the subject of this book.

Farscape the TV series relates the adventures of a wildly diverse mix of characters from a multitude of cultures as they traverse a corner of the universe known as the Uncharted Territories, struggling to stay one step ahead of all-too-persistent evil. The book you hold in your hand relates the *behind the scenes* adventures of another wildly diverse mix of characters from a multitude of cultures, traversing their own uncharted territories, also struggling to stay one step (sometimes barely half a step) ahead of disaster. Namely, the people who started it all, and who are responsible for the twenty-two hour episodes of the show's first year of production.

In addition to the vital creative participants mentioned and interviewed for this book, there are a few important players who were part of the earliest development of the series who remain unsung — and shouldn't. A special thank you to Alex Rockwell, Henson Company executive and producer, who championed the series and was in the trenches from the very beginning; Kirk Thatcher, part of the Henson Company creative team, who brainstormed with Alex and me as the series was first percolating; Luc Mayrand, conceptual artist extraordinaire, who was the first imagemaker I sat with, and was an important early collaborator on the visual interpretation of what such a series might look like; Bill Haber, one of the founders of Creative Artists Agency and someone who believed in this project and just wouldn't give up; and last but far from least...

David Kemper. Okay, as my fellow executive producer, David is interviewed extensively for this book, and his extreme significance to the series is well known. But here and now I must again give a big shout out to my collaborator, partner, protector, and friend. I remember one particular Sunday in 1994 when I was working up concepts for what would come after the première episode and David came over to my office and we talked for hours about all that the series could be. Not just any Sunday, but *Super Bowl Sunday*. David, I have one thing to say to you: the Cowboys won that day. And so did *Farscape*.

And one final thanks — to you, the fans of the series. With the advent of the Internet, networks have a direct and immediate means of gauging the intensity of fan interest in a particular series. You all have certainly made your voices heard, loud and clear.

This book is yours.

Enjoy.

Rockne S. O'Bannon
Los Angeles, July 2000

Opposite page: Early conceptual art for Pilot.

Above: *Series creator Rockne S. O'Bannon.*

Brian Henson, chairman of The Jim Henson Company

"For our first foray into science fiction, we were determined to do something that was truly exciting. The characters and the stories are, and continue to be, of the utmost importance – and we're delighted that they turned out to be every bit as wonderful and compelling as the astonishing special effects."

In the mid 1960s, Captain Kirk, Mr Spock and the brave crew of the USS *Enterprise* boldly went where no man had gone before, and changed the face of television science fiction. In 1993, nearly thirty years after Gene Roddenberry had overseen the production of *Star Trek*'s first episode at the Desilu Studios in Hollywood, Brian Henson and Rockne S. O'Bannon met to discuss what eventually would become *Farscape*. Ironically, this meeting also took place at Desilu Studios — since renamed Raleigh Studios — the former home of the Jim Henson Company.

From the very start, *Farscape* was going to be different from any other show. Elsewhere in Hollywood, *Star Trek: Deep Space Nine* and *Babylon 5* had just been launched. Chris Carter was creating *The X-Files*, and Teri Hatcher and Dean Cain were flying high in *Lois and Clark: The New Adventures of Superman*. Henson elaborates on *Farscape*'s genesis: "We wanted it to be more alien than any other television series — bolder, more emotional — and to have stronger, richer characters than on other SF shows. We knew we needed a concept that allowed the characters to be a little more dialled up."

After several months of discussion, Henson realised that he needed someone who knew how to bring humanity to science fiction. That someone was Rockne S. O'Bannon, whose work on the revival of *The Twilight Zone* and the 1988 movie *Alien Nation* had established him as a screenwriter able to produce science fiction that was more than just spaceships and lasers.

"I had a call from my agent, Bill Haber, who also used to represent the Henson Company," O'Bannon remembers. "Brian was looking for a television series that would really show all the facets of what the Henson Company could do in terms of developing animatronic characters, and also the then very young industry of computer generated imagery. He had a darker, more adult point of view than was traditional for the Henson Company. They wanted to do something on board a ship that had an animal team — a more *Star Wars*-like series. They had no idea who the characters were or anything like that, but basically said that they could bring some animatronic characters into this equation on television in a way that, obviously, *Star Trek* could not. So I went away and came up with the basic notion of the show. We all

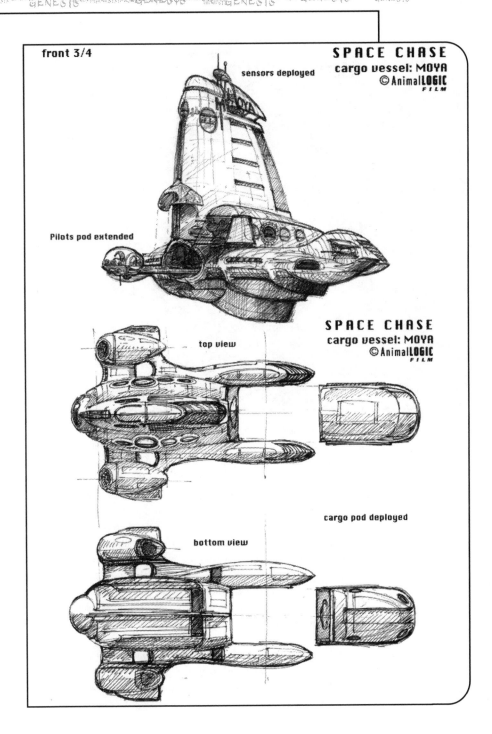

front 3/4

sensors deployed

SPACE CHASE
cargo vessel: MOYA
© Animal LOGIC
FILM

Pilots pod extended

SPACE CHASE
cargo vessel: MOYA
© Animal LOGIC
FILM

top view

cargo pod deployed

bottom view

want to be Gene Roddenberry, so the idea of doing a ship show had always intrigued me, but I had never really given it a great deal of thought.

"I came back and told them my notions. At that point, definitely in place, was the idea that it would be very dissimilar from *Star Trek*. Rather than have the *Star Trek* military hierarchy and all that, it would be a situation of anarchy. The crowning glory of the idea, which is sustained to this moment, is the concept of a man from our time dropped into the middle of this world at the other end of the universe. There's nothing else that does that. *Star Trek* takes place 500 years in the future, and *Star Wars* was 'a long time ago'. Buck Rogers falls asleep and wakes up in a future time. The idea of *Farscape* is taking essentially any one of us, and dropping us into *Star Wars*. John Crichton has *seen Star Wars*; he's seen all the *Star Trek* films. He's seen all the same television shows, movies, books and all those things that we all know, like *Monty Python*, and can bring that to bear on the world that he's in."

Farscape now moved into development. Or rather, *Space Chase* did, as the name *Farscape* wasn't chosen until 1998, very close to when filming began. In order to help sell the series to a network, who would broadcast the programme and provide the money for the Henson Company to make the episodes, Jamie Courtier of the Creature Shop was brought in to create a conceptual presentation. Drawings were prepared, and after discussions with Brian Henson and Rockne S. O'Bannon, maquettes (miniature sculptures) of the various characters were made, along with models of the spaceships that might populate this part of the universe.

Space Chase was conceived as an even more complex animatronic project than *Farscape* turned out to be. D'Argo was initially a much more lionesque being with, as O'Bannon recalls, "an animatronic head, but that would have been impossible on a TV series schedule, and we didn't want to do that with a regular character." There were plans to have a robot on board Moya, which Jamie Courtier remembers being envisaged as a comic character. Zhaan was conceived as a rotund man. Scorpius, an insect-like character with claws and mandibles, would have been a regular. Of the Creature Shop-created regulars, only Rygel and Pilot made it to the screen in their original form — except for a change of colour scheme and control panels.

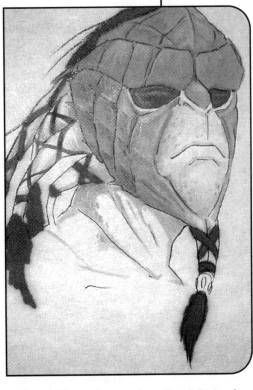

Page 9: Some early designs for Moya, featuring Farscape's *original title,* Space Chase.

Left and above: Concept sketches for D'Argo show his evolution from a more lionesque being.

Henson and O'Bannon took their presentation to the Fox Network, which in autumn 1993 was trying to establish itself as the fourth major network in America, alongside ABC, CBS and NBC. Fox was interested enough to ask for a pilot — a try-out episode — to see if what looked great on paper would actually work on screen. But *Space Chase* was going to be an expensive show to produce. It involved live actors, aliens prepared and operated by the Creature Shop, and all kinds of special effects. Everything — even simple things like knives and forks — had to be invented from scratch, which all cost money.

While the Henson Company would have loved the opportunity to shoot an hour of television to prove the viability of *Space Chase*, it was impossible to do so without funding. At that time, Fox would only have ordered six episodes, but the Henson Company would need money for eleven episodes to cover their costs. Fox wasn't prepared to go that far, but did offer development money to produce four more scripts, which would demonstrate other aspects of the show's potential, and take the Creature Shop designs a stage further.

During this period, O'Bannon was sharing his office with a fellow writer, David Kemper, who had been the CBS network executive assigned to O'Bannon's first professional writing job, *The Twilight Zone*, in 1985. The two men had remained good friends ever since and, now a freelance writer himself, Kemper was delighted to help on the project. At this time, Kemper was working on the season finale of *seaQuest DSV*, a series that O'Bannon had created for Steven Spielberg's Amblin Television, and was also in the midst of writing an episode for the new *Star Trek* series, *Voyager*, which would début the following spring. "We met up on Super Bowl Sunday," Kemper recalls. "I had the flu and Rockne had this office with a gas heater against the floor and I was shivering. We turned the heat on, and I was sitting up against the heater trying to get warm. We ended up doing five hours, coming up with a bunch of stories — and I missed the Super Bowl. It's the first Super Bowl I've ever missed. I said, 'Oh, man, this had better be worth it...'"

Though the four stories that O'Bannon and Kemper created — 'Awakening Dragons', 'Instinct for Survival', 'The Light of Truth' and 'Into the Lion's Den' — didn't end up on screen in their original form, elements from them, such as the Aurora Chair and Scorpius, appeared in *Farscape*'s first season, and 'The Light of Truth' was rewritten for the second season.

With these four scripts now ready (in addition to the original pilot script), O'Bannon and Henson returned to Fox in June 1994, hoping for a green light. Unfortunately, a change of executives at Fox meant that the project no longer had a champion. Undeterred, they tried elsewhere. "We pitched to Bob Iger and his top people at the ABC network," O'Bannon says, "and everybody liked what they saw. But again, everybody was just terribly afraid — 'Can this show really be made?' — because what we were presenting was really daunting. To be candid, science-fiction television has never really found success on regular television networks. The appeal isn't general enough."

ABC turned it down, so Henson and O'Bannon returned to Fox, and pitched to the man at the very top — Rupert Murdoch himself. However, in the intervening period, Fox had committed to another science-fiction series, the short-lived *Space: Above and Beyond*, from *The X-Files* writers Glen Morgan and James Wong. It looked as if this was the end for *Space Chase*.

But Henson was determined not to let the concept die. While O'Bannon went on to other projects, Henson and Marcy Ross, former senior vice president, creative affairs, continued to pitch the series. "Our presentation package — drawings of characters and interiors, models, a sort of representation of what this world might be — went on a slow march around the world for about three years," Jamie Courtier recalls. "Every now and then somebody would ask, 'Do

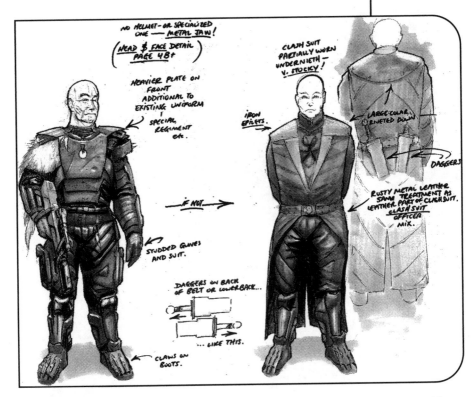

Above: One of the several early costume designs for Scorpius.

you know where the *Space Chase* maquettes are?' So we'd find them in Los Angeles or New York and then dispatch them."

"Every once in a while we'd go out and talk to people about it," O'Bannon recalls, "but what we were suggesting as a weekly series was always too daunting." Brian Henson takes up the story: "We started to re-work the series for an off-network approach and though we didn't actually think it was something that the SCI FI Channel could afford, luckily they were very ambitious in their thinking."

Rod Perth, president of SCI FI Channel, had received two of O'Bannon's scripts, and excitedly told his wife that he had found what he was looking for. At the same time, the Henson Company was trying to find co-production finance outside America. As discussions continued with the SCI FI Channel, another key player entered the *Farscape* story — Australian film and television producer Matt Carroll, who eventually produced the first season. Carroll had worked with Angus Fletcher, Henson's senior vice president, head of international television, on an Australian-English co-production some years earlier and asked Fletcher whether the show could be produced Down Under within the budget available.

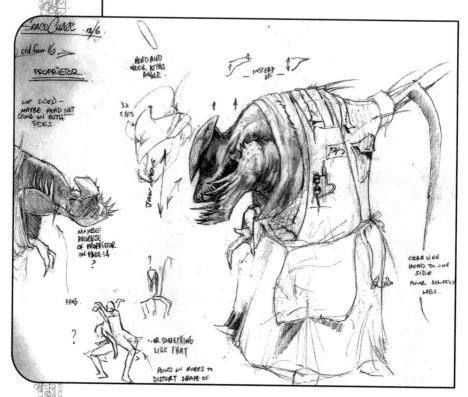

Carroll was responsible for bringing an Australian network into the production, so, ultimately, *Farscape* was made by a consortium of three companies: The Jim Henson Company, Hallmark Entertainment (the Henson Company's regular coproduction partner, and the makers of the major miniseries *Gulliver's Travels, Merlin,* and *The 10th Kingdom*) and Nine Films and Television, the production company division of the Australian Nine Network. "I just kept putting through ways of how we could structure it so it could be made in Australia," Carroll says. "It was an ideal project for Australia because we could make it for the budget that they had. So the project wasn't compromised at all in terms of the way Rockne envisaged it."

"I was excited at the prospect," O'Bannon recalls. "I liked the idea of the show looking as unusual as possible, and I knew that with American-influenced scripts but Australian directors, and all production and post-production entirely done in Australia, that we might get something that didn't look like any show that we've seen before. It wasn't an easy sell initially to the SCI FI Channel. The way I posed it was — if you look back at the original *Star Wars*, it had a very American-influenced story style, but because it was shot in England, the supporting players and just the *look* of it was not what audiences

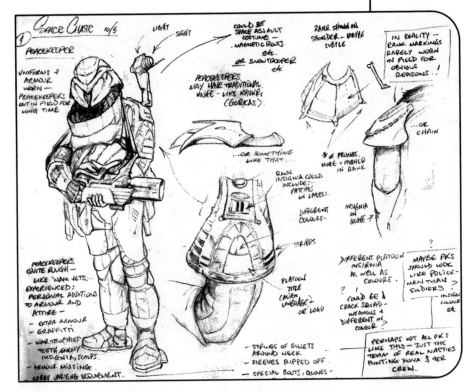

had come to expect from fully American productions."

Like O'Bannon and Henson, David Kemper was also unwilling to give up on *Space Chase*. "When a show dies in Hollywood it dies, and every year my agent said, '*Space Chase* is dead.' I said, 'No, no, Brian's going to try to sell it.' So in every contract thereafter I had a clause: if *Space Chase* ever started, I could walk off the show I was on.

"I was working on *Pacific Blue* in October of '97 and I got a call from Rock, saying, 'You're not going to believe this, I think we've sold the show.' So, I waited until it was official, in January '98, and then I had my agent call the people I was working with. So I was out of *Pacific Blue* and I was on *Space Chase*. Rock and I had already been in meetings from October '97 through to December. In January '98, we went to Australia. He started to rewrite the pilot script, and I started working on ideas for the season. In February, Rock and I started on these ideas ourselves, and on 1 May full pre-production began. And the day we started, we were already about four months behind!"

With Matt Carroll pulling together a behind-the-camera creative team from the cream of Australian talent, and with actors being auditioned on

Left and above: More early *Space Chase* concept sketches, for the Proprietor and a Peacekeeper soldier.

both sides of the Pacific for the leading roles, the final major change was put into place: the title *Farscape*. "We can do things that nobody else would do in their science-fiction series, and hopefully develop a unique tone — and that makes it *Farscape*," Brian Henson explains. "That's kind of why we needed to invent the word, too. We were thinking about different titles, and Rockne said, 'Let's invent a word, because if we want something that's truly unique, we probably can't describe the dynamic that we're talking about with any existing word that will say it's SF without creating some expectations.' Then, of course, none of us could agree on what the word should be. 'Parallax', that was a big one; there were eight or nine invented or obscure words we considered. But all of our broadcasters were really nervous about us making up a word — they asked, 'How do you market that?' But we were proven right. Our argument was: create a word, and that becomes the identity of the show. You can find it on the Internet — if you want to know about *Farscape*, you just do a search for that word, and all you will find is stuff about our show. You won't find a hundred thousand other things. You put in *Farscape*, you only get us."

The last word on the genesis of the series goes to David Kemper: "Brian Henson did something that people don't do in this business. You work for big companies, and they're institutions. A project dies, and it dies. Your executives go and hire other writers, they create something else. But Brian, stunningly, had a passion for this show, and because it was a family-owned company, with him in charge, no one was telling him, 'You have to let go of your dream.' So Brian held on to his dream, and Brian made the show go. There's a lot of people that there'd be no *Farscape* without, but in the very beginning there'd be no *Farscape* if Brian Henson hadn't held on for five years and said, 'I'm going to make *Farscape*. I don't care what they tell me, who gets in my way, how the obstacles are thrown, I'm not letting the show die.' Rock and I, we had to go off and make a living. Brian made a living too, but he never let go, and obviously he was right. Son of a gun, he sold it! There's no *Farscape* if Rock doesn't write any scripts, but boy, there would be no *Farscape* if Brian Henson hadn't gone back and sold what was essentially a dead project, and resurrected it. Brian *knew* that he could produce a good show, and he made it live through that act of dedication." ■

Left: *The cast, during the filming of the première episode.*

Above: *Brian Henson on set, directing the episode 'Exodus from Genesis'.*

THE EPISODES

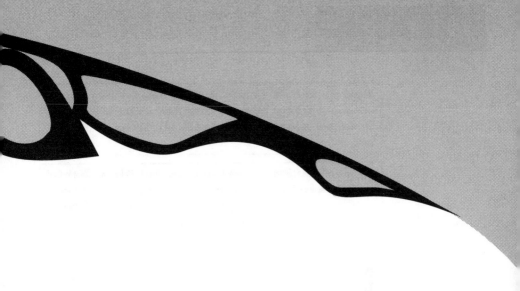

"My name is John Crichton, an astronaut. A radiation wave hit and I got shot through a wormhole. Now I'm lost in some distant part of the universe on a ship, a living ship, full of strange alien life forms. Help me. Help me. Listen, please. Is there anybody out there who can hear me? I'm being hunted by an insane military commander. Help me... Help me... I'm just looking for a way home."

Regular cast: Ben Browder (Commander John Crichton), Claudia Black (Officer Aeryn Sun), Anthony Simcoe (Ka D'Argo), Virginia Hey (Pa'u Zotoh Zhaan), John Eccleston (Dominar Rygel XVI: movement), Jonathan Hardy (Dominar Rygel XVI: voice), Sean Masterson (Pilot: movement), Lani Tupu (Pilot: voice)

Written by: Rockne S. O'Bannon **Directed by:** Andrew Prowse	**Guest cast:** Lani Tupu (Captain Bialar Crais), Kent McCord (Jack Crichton), Murray Bartlett (DK), Christine Stephen-Daly (Lt Teeg), Damen Stephenson (Bio Isolation Man #1), Colin Borgonon (PK Weapons Officer)

uring an experimental mission in Earth's orbit, Commander John Crichton's craft, *Farscape 1*, hits an unexpected electromagnetic wave. The ship is sucked through a wormhole and spat out in a distant part of the universe — right into the middle of a pitched space battle. Having accidentally collided with another spacecraft, which results in the death of its pilot, Tauvo Crais, *Farscape 1* is drawn through an intake port on Moya, a huge bio-mechanoid Leviathan ship. Moya's crew are recently escaped prisoners — Luxan warrior Ka D'Argo, Delvian priest Pa'u Zotoh Zhaan and deposed Hynerian Dominar, Rygel XVI — all on the run from the Peacekeepers, a vast mercenary force with powerful influence across thousands of systems. To escape from the Peacekeepers, Moya uses a risky StarBurst hyperspace manoeuvre, which inadvertently traps a Peacekeeper ship, flown by Officer Aeryn Sun, inside its energy envelope. Brought onboard the ship, Aeryn is put in a cell with Crichton. While Moya's crew locates a Commerce planet, searching for iriscentant fluid for Moya and provisions for themselves, Crichton and Aeryn escape from their cell. The Peacekeeper contacts her superior officer — Captain Bialar Crais, Tauvo's brother. The captain now has a personal vendetta against Crichton, whom he holds responsible for his brother's death, while Aeryn is deemed "irreversibly contaminated" after her contact with the human...

Crichton

"Hey Dad. It worked. DK's and my theory. It actually worked, sort of... Technically I don't know how I got here, but I'm not going to stop trying to get home."

"When writing's good, it plays itself," guest star Kent McCord recalls of his pivotal role as John Crichton's father, Jack, in the première episode. "All I had to do was deliver what the writer had written and believe the moment." *Farscape* series creator Rockne S. O'Bannon welcomed the casting of the veteran actor. "It was just wonderful to see a comfortable, familiar face, and a pro," he says. "It got us off to a good start."

Director Andrew Prowse remembers the discussions about ensuring the

audience identified with John Crichton as he encountered the weird and wonderful world that was to become his home. "One of the reasons for the success of *Farscape*," says Prowse, "is we've always put the human drama first. If you have one human in a land full of aliens, then your only access is through that human. He has to be the centre; you've got to see things through his eyes. The aliens can only be understood through human experience. You've got to put that right up front."

Visual-effects supervisor Paul Butterworth notes that the first episode of any SF series is the most difficult, since everything has to be made from scratch. According to Henson Creature Shop production designer Ricky Eyres, the design of Crichton's experimental ship is closer to scientific fact than science fiction. "It was actually modelled on an experimental re-entry craft that NASA was working on," he says.

Another of Eyres's most striking designs was created for the Peacekeepers. "I felt like they should be the Nazis in space," says Eyres, "but that's been done a lot, so we put a different slant on it. Predominantly the colour scheme is black and red, which is Nazi, but I'm a big fan of the Russian constructivist style, and when you combine those two schools you get a very strong identity, and a powerful look."

Above: The launch of Farscape 1.

Next page: Crichton suggests a daring manoeuvre to escape Crais.

Eyres has one regret about the finished episode: "We never properly established the scale of the Peacekeeper Command Carrier. There were a couple of shots missing, because of certain restrictions on the CG. We needed to establish that the Carrier was 5,000 feet long, which is three times the size of Moya, but I don't think people got that."

Composer Chris Neal, who with his son, Braedy, records and performs under the collective name 'Subvision' — recalls the genesis of *Farscape*'s distinctive theme music. "If Matt Carroll, Brian Henson and Rockne O'Bannon had insisted that we give them *Star Wars*, that's what we would have given them," he admits, "but the brief was 'somewhere between tribal and medieval,' and they said, 'It's up to you guys to make it work for outer space.' It was a wonderful brief, and when we came up with the theme, they just said, 'Bingo — you've done it!'" Initially, the network did not feel the same way. "They hated it," Neal recalls. "They really did not want to go with a female vocal, but we just kept fighting for it, because we felt that we had to have some sort of yearning sound, a tribal feel, because that's the whole point of *Farscape*. Moya's a female, there's a strong female presence in the cast, and there are all these people trying to find their way home." Fortunately, he adds, "everybody in the production felt so strongly about it that they all uniformly resisted the network."

In fact, the soundtrack to the première episode was nominated for a Golden Reel Award which, Neal explains, "is recognition for a total soundtrack: dialogue, music, effects, the whole soundscape. We were nominated with *The X-Files* and *E.R.*, so we were in great company." ■

THRONE FOR A LOSS

Written by: Richard Manning	**Guest cast:** John Adam (Bekhesh), Jeremiah Tickell (Kyr),
Directed by: Pino Amenta	Zoe Dimakis (Hontovek), Api Bavadra (Nonk)

t Rygel's suggestion, a delegation of Tavleks from a nearby planet are invited aboard Moya. The crew hope to get a good price for transporting some of the Tavleks' cargo. However, without the others' knowledge, Rygel 'borrows' a gem-like crystalline component from Moya's propulsion system, in an effort to impress the Tavleks with his wealth. Far from being the peaceful traders he thinks, the Tavleks are, in fact, ruthless warriors, each equipped with a gauntlet which administers a powerful, aggression-heightening stimulant, and acts as a deadly weapon. Launching a surprise attack on the crew, the Tavleks kidnap Rygel. As a crippled Moya sets off in pursuit, Aeryn interrogates a Tavlek who was left behind. D'Argo — now sporting a Tavlek gauntlet — becomes uncontrollably aggressive, despite Zhaan's attempt to subdue him with a "sleep mist." A ransom demand is soon received from Bekhesh, the Tavlek leader, who believes Rygel's phony claims of vast wealth. To infiltrate the Tavlek camp and rescue Rygel, Crichton will need the gauntlet D'Argo is wearing — but must knock him out to get it. Even imprisoned, the Hynerian behaves in his usual arrogant manner, regaling his cellmate, Jotheb, with grandiose stories, and never considering what will happen when his captors find out he is not the wealthy monarch he claims to be.

> **Crichton**
>
> "That's your plan? Wile E. Coyote would come up with a better plan than that!"

'Throne for a Loss' was a real challenge for Henson's creature-effects supervisor Dave Elsey, whose department had to create two entirely new species for the show — the Tavleks and the Trao. Costume designer Terry Ryan worked with Elsey on the concept for the Tavleks: "Basically, they're a nomadic species going from one place to another, just looting and getting everything they can. They had this fantastic armour, and we tried to make it look as if it were made from some kind of stone or other foreign material, not

ENCOUNTERS: TAVLEKS

A race of battle-scarred warriors whose exceptional aggression, strength, endurance and fighting prowess is fuelled by a constant supply of a powerful and highly addictive stimulant injected into their forearms by armoured gauntlets, which also act as energy weapons. Although savage scavengers by nature, their trade in all manner of stolen goods is supplemented by kidnapping and extortion.

something we humans would use for armour. In fact, it was only rubber."

Elsey has this to say about his design for the Tavlek leader: "The idea was that he had been in a battle where he'd had the top of his head blown off, and had replaced it with some sort of found technology. So he basically had a fibreglass headpiece on, and the actor was looking out through the dents, bullet holes and screw holes. That worked incredibly well."

A more complicated construction was the character of Jotheb, "next in succession to preside over the Collective of Trao," a large, multi-tentacled and multi-larynxed creature. "With him, we were told that we could do anything we liked, because we were never going to see him properly," Elsey recalls. "But I've been doing this long enough to know that if ever they say, 'You'll never see it,' you always do!" Jotheb was operated by putting a false floor in the cell next to Rygel's, so that the puppeteer would be up to his waist inside the complicated Jotheb rig. "That way, it looks as though he's got this really stunted little body. All the tentacles were on wires and cables — really low-tech stuff," Elsey points out, "but the suit was actually very complicated."

Director Pino Amenta had a hand in introducing the show's comic edge with this episode. "Things like, 'Wile E. Coyote would come up with a

better plan' weren't in the script," says Ben Browder. "Pino would go, 'What else would Crichton say? How about Wile E. Coyote?'" Virginia Hey remembers 'Throne for a Loss' marking another first: an indication of Zhaan's dark side. "The Tavleks are all drug addicts, and when one comes aboard, Zhaan reaches out to him," she recalls. "The way it was written, Zhaan was actually quite calm and gentle. But, at one point, she just grabs him, twists his arm behind his back, and slams him onto the desk because, as Zhaan, I became impatient with him and his games. According to the executive producer, David Kemper, that was the first thing that made him think, 'Ah, of course, she has a strong side!'"

At six foot three, Hey says that Zhaan's physical strength seemed to go comfortably, if paradoxically, with her spiritual strength. "I wanted Zhaan to be more physical, because although I'm not exactly athletic, I am a strong person, and I suppose that after all that time of being very pious and gentle, you want to break free, and lash out! So, Zhaan's intolerance was written into that script, but I think I took it a bit further. The writers flew with it, and eventually they came across her dark side..." ■

Opposite page: The Tavlek gauntlet weapon.

Above: *Crichton with Bekhesh, the Tavlek leader.*

BACK AND BACK AND BACK
TO THE FUTURE

| Written by: Babs Greyhosky | Guest cast: John Clayton (Verell), Lisa Hensley (Matala) |
| Directed by: Rowan Woods | |

Moya comes across a damaged ship in the midst of subatomic disintegration. Rygel and D'Argo want nothing to do with it, until a distress signal from the vessel reveals the occupants to be Ilanics — a race genetically related to Luxans, and with whom they have a treaty. D'Argo insists on bringing the single survival pod from the stricken ship aboard Moya with its two surviving crewmembers, a scientist, Verell, and his female assistant, Matala. While checking the pod, Crichton is wounded by a subatomic discharge from the Ilanic ship, and begins having wild sexual hallucinations — or perhaps premonitions — involving Matala. Verell claims that their cruiser was studying deep space gravitational fluctuations when its core regulator began malfunctioning (in fact, they are transporting a tiny particle of a black hole). Although Zhaan doubts their story, D'Argo offers to take them and their precious data to their destination. After learning that Matala has had Scorvian training, Aeryn distrusts her, as does Crichton — especially after having premonitions in which Matala murders Verell, D'Argo and himself. Matters are not helped by D'Argo's attraction to Matala, and his irrational urge to protect her, or by Crichton's attempts to alter the future...

> **Zhaan to Crichton**
>
> "Premonitions. Future flashes. The concept is a fascinating one."
>
> "Yeah, well, it could just still be a concept. I could just be going plain old bonkers here."

"I'm just a huge fan of Rowan Woods," says Ben Browder of the regular *Farscape* director who joined the series with this episode. "He brought a dark sensibility to the show, and at the same time he is funny and twisted. We were discussing the flash-forwards at the beginning of that

ENCOUNTERS: ILANICS AND SCORVIANS

The Ilanics are a bipedal species with cranial tentacles, distant genetic cousins of the Luxans, with whom they have been blood allies for over a thousand cycles. They have been at war with the Scorvians for three cycles, ever since the Scorvians attacked an outlying colony of Ilanics, and slaughtered two million civilians. Ruthless warriors, the Scorvians are so committed to wiping out the Ilanics that their agents genetically alter themselves to infiltrate Ilanic ships. Little more is known about the species, beyond that they possess a deadly attack known as the 'Scorvian neural stroke'.

episode," Browder recalls. "The scene has Matala having sex with Crichton, and it was written as a straight titillation sort of thing. But Rowan said, 'No, I think it's like a kind of dark sexual fantasy.' I said, 'Okay,' and instead of being anything romantic or mushy, the episode suddenly takes a dark twist, which is perfectly true to the script. If you're sitting in the room, and suddenly you're having this image of you having sex with an alien, you're *not* going to have a really excited reaction. You're going to have an, 'Oh my God, what is happening?' reaction."

Claudia Black recalls the scope that the script offered the director: "Rowan had an opportunity to create that sense, which I think is very much a part of science fiction, of constantly being able to turn the story on its head, and let the audience keep guessing where it's going." Black was also enthralled by her fight scene, which reminded her of the start of a video game: "The two characters who are sparring face each other, and then the camera angle sweeps down from the crane and catches them in profile before they commence fighting."

There were other artistic influences on the fight scene. Ricky Eyres explains: "Russian constructivism was a form of art that developed before the revolution. There was a famous painting called 'Beat the Whites with

Above: Matala and Verell.

Next page: Crichton is caught up in sub-atomic discharge from the Ilanic ship.

the Red Witch', and there's one blatant piece of it in this episode, which you see when Aeryn's fighting with Matala. It starts with an overhead crane shot, and it's actually that painting, broken down as a carpet. It just seemed to fit, and from a visual point of view it was very strong."

Pete Coogan, production executive for The Jim Henson Company, also admired Rowan Woods's direction of the cast. "That was one of my favourites," Coogan recalls. "The scene with Zhaan's death mask, and Crichton reciting what has happened — they were stunning. Rowan really pulls the performances out of the actors." No wonder the episode is also one of the cast's favourites. "I really enjoyed watching Ben explore his character's twists and turns," Virginia Hey remembers. "He was like a kid with a new toy! It's lovely to be involved in such magic."

The strange, gravity warping effects of the black hole and the explosions presented certain challenges for the visual-effects department. "It was a busy story for us, obviously," Paul Butterworth recalls. "We had to do a lot of warping, to get the effect of the Ilanic ship being crushed down to next to nothing, and then come up with ways of making it explode convincingly. We used a lot of off-the-shelf explosions and elements to try and get that sense of scale." ■

I, E.T.

Written by: Sally Lapiduss Directed by: Pino Amenta	Guest cast: Mary Mara (Lyneea), Cayde Tasker (Fostro), Boris Brkic (Commander Ryymax), Mark Shaw (Alien Soldier#1), Dominic Bianco (Alien Hunter#1), Heath Wilder (Alien Hunter#2)

T he removal of Moya's Control Collar belatedly triggers the Paddac Beacon — an alarm buried deep within her neural nexus, emitting a powerful tracking signal which will alert any nearby Peacekeepers to the escaped ship's whereabouts. Although Pilot manages to shut off the aural component of the siren, the beacon continues to broadcast. Figuring that water may help to muffle the external signal, Crichton suggests landing Moya in the swampland of a nearby planet, which looks, according to Crichton, "kinda like Louisiana." The first problem is that no one knows whether a Leviathan can actually land on a planet's surface — or take off again. The second problem: to effect a permanent shut-down, the tracking device must be physically cut out of Moya, a procedure which will cause her intolerable pain. To numb her, the crew must locate some Clorium, one of the six forbidden cargoes. The situation is made even more perilous because Moya's arrival has been detected by some local inhabitants, who have never encountered alien life. Aeryn and D'Argo create a diversion so Crichton can search for the Clorium, but before he finds it, he falls into the hands of an inquisitive little nine year old boy...

> **Crichton**
>
> "We can stick our heads between our legs and kiss our asses goodbye! It's a *saying...*"

'I, E.T.' was part of the second batch of episodes to be filmed back-to-back. Originally, it was intended to be broadcast as the second episode in the season, but the decision was made to move it back in the running order for the show's airing on the SCI FI Channel in America. "It's such an unusual show," series creator O'Bannon explains, "that there were those at the SCI FI Channel who were not confident about airing it that

ENCOUNTERS: DENEANS

Dwellers of a small, Earth-like planet, the Deneans possess technology similar to Earth's. Though they seem somewhat primitive to Aeryn and D'Argo, Crichton feels more at home on this planet than he has anywhere else. Deneans have never encountered alien life before the arrival of Moya's crew, and while the scientist Lyneea is ecstatic to make 'first contact', the military forces are not so welcoming, suggesting their behaviour is similar to Earth's military.

early, and the network was very cautious about what order they would show it in."

This means that sharp-eyed Scapers can spot what appears to be an error in the continuity. In 'Throne for a Loss' and 'Back and Back and Back to the Future', Aeryn is gradually becoming more at ease with the other members of Moya's crew. However, in 'I, E.T.', she reverts to behaving more like a Peacekeeper, and wonders why she is helping former prisoners. Claudia Black says that the discrepancy is unfortunate in terms of her character's arc. "If they shuffle the order," she notes, "it runs the risk of jarring the audience's perception of the storytelling and what has happened to the characters." But sometimes that cannot be helped. David Kemper points out that 'PK Tech Girl' actually aired before the première, as a sneak preview. Besides, he adds, "It plays better to go from a ship-based episode to a planet-based episode, as opposed to having ship, ship, planet, planet."

At this early stage of the season's production, the various departments were all working very closely together. "At the start of it," Ricky Eyres recalls, "myself, costume designer Terry Ryan, make-up supervisor Lesley Vanderwalt and creature-effects supervisor Dave Elsey were very tight, and

there was always harmony. The speed we were working at, we'd all be thinking about the same thing without us actually talking about it. You only get the script two days before you shoot, so two weeks before that, we're actually working on an episode without a finished script."

Moya's crash-landing into the swamp was a new challenge for Paul Butterworth's visual-effects department. "We had particle explosions of water which spray in all directions," he recalls, "and we had to do 3D water, which is always difficult in CG. Anything that has natural movement — like smoke, fire, wind and water — is always really hard to develop. Essentially, I wanted to blow up a large section of water for real — but that was never going to happen, so we had to generate it all in 3D."

"To this day I remain a fan of this episode," says O'Bannon. "Because it was one of the first episodes shot, it suffered somewhat in execution, but the concept of John Crichton finding himself as an 'alien' in a world not dissimilar to Earth was an important step in establishing a tone for the series that was vital. After the première episode, Crichton could have easily fallen into that cocky, nothing-really-matters TV hero category, *à la* Buck Rogers. But in 'I, E.T.' there's a level of melancholy and longing for home in John's reactions to this planet, and to the character played so well by Mary Mara, that served as a tonal touchstone for the writers of all the episodes that followed." ■

Opposite page: Crichton befriends the young Denean Fostro.

Above: D'Argo is captured by the Denean military.

Written by: Ro Hume	**Guest cast:** Damian de Montemas (Melkor), Jodie Dry
Directed by: Brian Henson	(Kyona), Geoff Barker (PK Commando #3), Chenoeh Miller
	(PK Commando #4), Tai Scrivener (PK Commando #5)

Moya is being scanned by a Marauder — a Peacekeeper vessel crewed by crack commandos, serving Crais's Command Carrier — hidden on the opposite side of what appears to be an asteroid nebula. But the nebula is actually a swarm of insectoid life forms known as Draks, several hundred of which invade Moya. The Draks increase the on-board temperature to a level that is uncomfortable for most of the crew, but may be fatal to Aeryn whose species is unusually sensitive to heat. As Aeryn begins to slip into Heat Delirium — the first stage of the dreaded 'Living Death' which turns Sebaceans into zombies — Crichton discovers that the Draks also can create physically and genetically identical replicas of each of the crew members. Aeryn makes Crichton promise to kill her if she worsens, but if the Draks are making multiple copies of her — not to mention D'Argo, Zhaan and himself — how will he know which one to kill? The crew are desperate to rid Moya of the Draks, who continue to increase the temperature and also are preparing *something* behind a sealed door. What's more, the Marauder is still searching the area, and Moya is in no position to flee...

> ### Aeryn to Crichton
>
> "I'm sure your world has no force so ruthless, so disciplined."
>
> "Oh, we call 'em line backers, or serial killers. Depends on whether they're professional or amateur."

Although broadcast fifth, 'Exodus from Genesis' was one of the two-part block of episodes filmed first (the other being 'Première'). The director was Brian Henson, now chairman of the Jim Henson Company, and Emmy award-winning director of several productions, including the films *Muppet Treasure Island* and *The Muppet Christmas Carol*. "Because that was the first

ENCOVNTERS: DRAKS

A species with a remarkable life cycle who can invade passing vessels. Two-foot long, blue-blooded, cockroach-like creatures who excrete a blue adhesive polymer, Draks have the ability to perfectly replicate any living creature from a DNA sample (except for the power of speech). Their complex reproductive cycle requires that they locate an extremely warm place in which their queen or Monarch can incubate their pod-like eggs. The Monarch can also infect another creature via a stinger and take over its body for a period of time, allowing her to communicate. Once the creatures are hatched, they return to space.

episode we shot, we tried to put a little bit of everything in it," recalls
Henson, adding that 'Exodus from Genesis' marked the steepest learning
curve of the entire series. Although this was made easier by the story taking
place entirely on Moya, Henson says that such 'bottle shows' are often his
favourite episodes. "Because the ship is this living being," he says, "it's
unpredictable how she works. The sets are big, spooky and mysterious,
and you never know what the next space you're gonna find is, or what
purpose it serves."

This early episode also gave some of the cast members a taste of the
varied experiences to come on *Farscape*. "The metamorphosis, for me, was
lovely to do," says Virginia Hey, remembering Zhaan's possession by the Drak
Monarch. "That was my first experiment with an *alter ego* — losing my own
personality and being taken over by another. It's my voice," she adds, referring
to the flat, alien sounds with which Zhaan speaks under the Monarch's influence, "but it's been doctored." Hey was less thrilled about the name which
American writer Ro Hume first gave to the Drak queen. "Originally, they called
her the sultana, because in America, a sultana is known as the wife of a sultan.
But in Australia, as in Britain, a sultana is the name of a bloody raisin! I was
saying, 'Don't call me a sultana, please, because I look a bit like a squashed

Above: A Drak
attacks.

Next page:
Examining the Drak
replica of Aeryn.

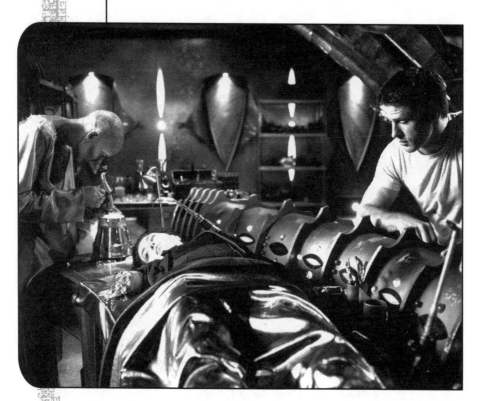

plum as it is!' So they changed the name of the queen to Monarch instead."

Visually, 'Exodus from Genesis' was an extremely complex episode, and filming it in tandem with 'Première' required the visual-effects crew to work flat out. "'Exodus' was incredibly difficult," Paul Butterworth recalls. "Trying to give CG particles the characteristics of a live swarm, is really hard, because particles are dumb from a computer point of view." The script presented other visual-effects challenges, such as the digital removal of the wires and rods used to operate the creatures. "It takes up huge amounts of computer time to do rig removal," producer Matt Carroll explains, "because you've got to do it frame by frame."

The biggest task in this respect, Carroll recalls, was when the creatures are first seen in Crichton's quarters. Series creator O'Bannon remembers the development of this scene, and how he stressed the importance of ensuring Crichton's reactions to alien phenomena were always realistic: "There are people who freak out if they see an ordinary cockroach — so if it's a massive cockroach, we'd be, like, 'What the…!' I said to the writers, 'Put yourself in a room with one of these things, and then a second one drops off the ceiling. How would *you* react?' Then it becomes quite natural." ∎

THANK GOD IT'S FRIDAY, AGAIN

Written by: David Wilks	**Guest cast:** Angie Milliken (Volmae), Ken Blackburn
Directed by: Rowan Woods	(Hybin), Tina Thomsen (Tanga), Selina Muller (D'Argo's
	Girlfriend), Mark Slocum (Sykaran Male #1), Peter Baroch
	(Sykaran Male #3)

In the grip of a Luxan Hyper Rage, D'Argo storms down to the sun-baked surface of the planet Sykar. After giving their shipmate a few days to cool off, the crew catches up with him on Sykar, only to find that not only has his Hyper Rage evaporated, but that he has become infatuated with a beautiful blonde Sykaran woman. D'Argo wishes to remain on her homeworld, helping to harvest the Tannot roots which are the life-blood of the Sykaran race. Crichton's suspicions are aroused by D'Argo's uncharacteristic behaviour, and heightened further when another native woman begs him to stay on Sykar. Meanwhile, Rygel discovers that something he ate whilst on the planet has made his bodily fluids somewhat... explosive. While Crichton and Zhaan remain on Sykar with D'Argo, Aeryn takes Rygel back to the ship, where his indigestion continues to produce fiery results. As Aeryn and Pilot work to cure Rygel, Crichton begins to wonder whether D'Argo's unusual behaviour and Rygel's illness could be linked to the effects of the Tannot root. If so, what can be done to reverse them — and what other secrets do the Sykarans hold?

> **Rygel to Aeryn**
>
> "I've suffered many assassination attempts on Hyneria, but..."
>
> "Nobody knows you here. It's only people who know you who want to kill you."

'Thank God It's Friday, Again' saw a memorably 'alien' performance from Angie Milliken, as Sykaran leader Volmae. Make-up supervisor Lesley Vanderwalt remembers her as "the one with the white head and the red eyes, and all that slow speaking. We were working in this big open shed and it was very dry. We had red contact lenses in her eyes, and in the first shot as she walked towards the camera, her eyes started flickering. I thought her contacts had dried out and they were going to slip out, but she ended up just using it as part of her performance."

ENCOUNTERS: SYKARANS

The maroon-skinned, blonde-haired and white-eyed inhabitants of Sykar were contented farmers until they were enslaved by Peacekeepers and forced to harvest Tannot roots, an alien plant which is used as part of the fuel for Peacekeeper weapons. Ingestion of the Tannot root turns the Sykarans into docile servants, but the few who are immune to the roots' effects may one day be enough to lead a revolution.

According to Terry Ryan, deciding on what costumes for the Sykarans should look like was a logical decision. "If you think of farmers," he explains, "they're always out working in the fields, so you'd give them all bleached hair and sun-tanned skin, and add a sort of cracking effect, because you're in this hot environment." As for Volmae, he says, "she was the white woman, who was always inside. She never went out in the sun, so we pushed it a bit — made the Sykarans a bit browner than they should be, and made Volmae very pale. The other thing with the Sykarans," he adds, "is that initially we talked about the fact that if you're really sun-tanned, you want to wear a white shirt to show it off. But these people want to wear red clothing to de-emphasise the suntan, but the sun has faded the fabrics into all those pinks and oranges. It also helps them to look better as a group."

The bold colour schemes influenced other members of the crew. "We call that the red episode, because of the costumes," says composer Chris Neal. "Initially, though, there was going to be a big emphasis on the trains, and we started off playing with railway-type themes. Once the episode was edited, and we saw that there was less footage of the trains, we went with a more Balinese influence — I guess we settled on 'Bali meets

Turkey' for that one. You can't specifically draw from one ethnicity, because then it's not *Farscape*. A lot of the time, it was difficult to define to ourselves what we actually meant by 'the *Farscape* style' of music, but we knew it when we heard it! Usually it was a combination of more than one theme."

The episode's subplot, Aeryn working with Pilot to find a cure for Rygel, gave Claudia Black an opportunity to start developing her character. "Aeryn was finding it really hard in that one," says Black. She was lost. I went into it thinking that Aeryn was like a robot who would become more human. I talked to the director, Rowan Woods, about it, and about how we were trying to let Aeryn grow." However, series creator O'Bannon was initially surprised at how Claudia played the scenes. "In my rewrite pass at the script, it was far more straightforward. Aeryn was openly uncomfortable... fumbling isn't quite the right word, but she was far less comfortable and trepidatious about doing science and all that. When I saw Claudia's performance, I was really aghast and I was thinking, 'Well, she really missed that!' Then, when it cut together, it was exactly what it should have been, because if she had gone where I had designed it, it wouldn't have given us all the distance for her character to go through the rest of the season." ■

Opposite page:
Harvesting the Tannot roots.

Above: D'Argo and Zhaan become willing servants of Volmae.

PK TECH GIRL

Written by: Nan Hagan Directed by: Tony Tilse	Guest cast: Alyssa-Jane Cook (Gilina Mays, PK Technician), Derek Amer (Teurac), Peter Astridge (Lomus), Peter Knowles (Evran), David Wheeler (Captain Selto Durka)

Moya detects a derelict ship floating in space. Upon closer examination, it is found to be the *Zelbinion*, the most feared ship in the Peacekeeper fleet, missing for around 100 cycles. For Rygel, it brings back terrible memories, as this was the ship upon which he was first tortured 130 cycles ago, by its dreaded captain, Durka. Crichton, D'Argo and Aeryn board the vessel, looking for galactic star-charts but find only the desiccated remains of several Peacekeepers. But there's another Peacekeeper onboard who's in somewhat better shape: pretty Peacekeeper technician Gilina Mays, who — having served on Crais's ship — recognises Aeryn and the escaped prisoners. Gilina tells how she was left on the *Zelbinion* with several others, to carry out tests. However, once Crais's ship had deserted them, they were invaded by scavenging Sheyangs, who killed her colleagues and stripped the ship of anything of value. Her story seems plausible — the evidence is all around them. Then Moya senses the Sheyang ship, and Gilina reveals that they are returning for the *Zelbinion's* Defence Shield which, although it isn't operational, is the least damaged part of the ship. While D'Argo and Zhaan keep the Sheyangs at bay, Crichton, Aeryn and Gilina race to get the shield working again…

> **D'Argo to Crichton**
>
> "This ship is legendary, even in my culture. It was thought invincible."
>
> "Yeah, well, just ask Leonardo Di Caprio - even the big ones go down."

Matt Carroll remembers 'PK Tech Girl' as a stylistic milestone in the development of the series. "We always talked euphemistically that *Farscape* lay somewhere between *Star Wars* and *Alien*. So, in other words, it wasn't the complete fantasy that *Star Wars* is — a sort of romantic, fantasy space world — and it wasn't as dark and grim as *Alien*. But it had to have an adventure edge that was somewhere in between those two. We found it in 'PK Tech Girl', and that really gave us a benchmark episode to work towards."

ENCOUNTERS: SHEYANGS

Slimy, ichthyosaur-type creatures who breathe bolts of fire which can reach oxy-acetylene temperatures. Scavengers by nature, Sheyangs roam the universe plundering derelict craft — many of which they've rendered useless themselves with their powerful plasma weapons. Exploiting weakness, afraid of strength, they are deeply fearful of Luxans.

But there are other reasons why 'PK Tech Girl' is one of the most important episodes of *Farscape*'s début season. It was the first show that was shot as a single episode, so that the director, cast and crew could concentrate on just one storyline, rather than dividing their attentions between two, as they had previously. "We were double-shooting episodes, and the quality was not what we wanted it to be," recalls David Kemper. It also marks the start of what Ben Browder describes as the 'Tilsification Factor' — the unique stamp that incoming director Tony Tilse brought to *Farscape*. "Tony is like a kid in a candy store or a toy shop," says Pete Coogan. "He would always have this incredible enthusiasm. The energy of his shows, I think, comes to the fore."

'PK Tech Girl' was also significant for being the first *Farscape* footage seen by the general public, shown as a USA Network sneak preview in the week immediately before the series' première on the SCI FI channel in March, 1999. Partly shot, like many first season episodes, at the White Bay nuclear power station near Sydney, it went through a number of plot changes. For instance, Gilina originally wasn't going to survive her stay on the *Zelbinion*, Kemper recalls: "I wanted a love story. I said, 'This isn't just a science-fiction show, it's a show about people.' As soon as I saw Alyssa-Jane, I had them rewrite the script to keep her alive, because I knew I was going

Above: The Sheyang Teurac appears on Moya's screen.

Next page: Crichton attempts to restore power to the Defence Shield.

to bring her back. You have this great love/romantic thing — why end it there? I said, 'We'll put her in a two-parter and kill her in that.' Which is what we did. You just see stuff and you start to weave a tapestry…"

As well as introducing the first proper love interest for John Crichton away from Moya, 'PK Tech Girl' also sees the début of another character destined to return: Rygel's nemesis, the Sebacean torturer, Durka. David Kemper admits that he wrote himself into a corner: "We have this actor who goes, 'Hello, Rygel, welcome home,' and I go, 'That's phenomenal! We have to use him again!' 'Well, he's dead,' I'm told. 'You killed him.' So we had to come up with a whole story of how and why he wasn't dead."

The main villains of the piece, however, are the Sheyangs — who are, in fact, making a return to the show. "We actually did a Sheyang in the very first episode," the Creature Shop's Dave Elsey reveals, "in the background on the Commerce planet talking to Zhaan. David Kemper saw it and said, 'Oh, these are so cool, I'm gonna write an episode for it.' I thought there's no reason why you can't come back to these things — there can be more of them on other planets, it makes the universe seem more real." ■

THAT OLD BLACK MAGIC

Written by: Richard Manning	Guest cast: Lani Tupu (Captain Bialar Crais), Chris
Directed by: Brendan Maher	Haywood (Maldis/IGG/Haloth), Grant Bowler (Liko),
	Christine Stephen-Daly (Lt Teeg)

While Rygel suffers aboard Moya with Klendian flu, the rest of the crew venture down to a primitive trading planet. As Zhaan searches for a cure for Rygel, Crichton meets a fortune-teller who seems to know many details about his personal life. Intrigued, Crichton agrees to follow him, but is instantly teleported to the home of Haloth, an elderly magician who knows even more about him. Haloth — in reality a powerful sorcerer named Maldis, who has subjugated the entire planet and its people — wrests Crichton's spirit from his body. Then he conjures Crais's spirit and pits the two against each other in a fight to the death. As Aeryn and D'Argo try to break into Maldis's complex, Zhaan and Liko, a local High Priest, combine their psychic powers in an effort to defeat Maldis. Crichton, whose unconscious body is found outside the fortune-teller's dwelling, is taken back to Moya, and left in Rygel's tender care...

> **Maldis to Crichton**
>
> "My name is Maldis. But you can address me as Haloth if you like. I got a lot of names, John Boy. Call me whatever pops your cork!"
>
> "Yeah, right. You're a regular Laurence Olivier."

With Maldis and his *alter egos*, the stage was set for one of the more theatrical *Farscape* stories. Visually, however, a cinematic influence came to bear. "There was a bit of a Ken Adam homage in that episode," explains Ricky Eyres, referring to the legendary set designer best known for his work on the James Bond films. "We try to steer away from using Earthbound styles, but there's a definite 1960s look to that one. The director Brendan Maher, and Chris Haywood, playing Maldis, were great. They both came up with a lot of ideas for the approach and style of the episode, which came out really well. Chris was so over the top, he was fantastic." Terry Ryan, who worked closely with Eyres on the episode, agrees. "It was partly the actor," he says, "but it was also that Maldis plays games — he

ENCOUNTERS: TRELKEZ

Brightly-coloured, bird-like creatures with two or more heads and a pitiful cry. The tender brains of the Trelkez are known to Sebaceans and many other species as a delicacy. Their value, therefore, depends on the number of heads each Trelkez possesses. As Crichton is somewhat disgusted to discover, they are never cooked, but always served raw.

dresses up as these different people, and each different sort of character that he plays is out of the dressing-up box."

"This is one of those episodes where Ricky Eyres's genius really shines," says O'Bannon. "Maldis's 'playground' is just a remarkable set — full of movement, bizarre textures, even fire! I originally pursued Ricky for *Farscape* because of his work on *The Young Indiana Jones Chronicles*, a series with an amazing scale and scope in terms of production design. 'That Old Black Magic' is a shining example of how a TV series can achieve sets of remarkable size and imagination: just hire a genius like Ricky Eyres."

According to Paul Butterworth, the confrontation between Crichton, Crais and Maldis in front of the pit of fire benefited from some behind-the-scenes additions. "I think the trickiest thing for us in that episode was a 'shot fix' that we had to do for the guys on set," he remembers. "We had to digitally add a lot more fire to the pit." That, he adds, turned out to be tricky, since the visual-effects house didn't have the necessary footage to splice seamlessly into the live action: "There was a lot of cutting and pasting from all over the place!" The visual-effects department was also responsible for the various magical elements that appeared throughout the episode. "A lot of

ideas were bounced around for that," Butterworth recalls, "because there were lots of different energy fields and auras, and no one really knew what they should be like."

Understandably, Lani Tupu sees 'That Old Black Magic' as a key episode for Crais, and for the Crichton/Crais relationship. "His childhood is taken away and he's conscripted into the Peacekeepers against his will," Tupu says of Crais's backstory. "The only way he can deal with that is to defy authority, and in doing that he's ostracised even more from the Peacekeeper community. But I think he likes that, because he never knows where that will lead, and that's changed him. He's not just following orders, which he has been doing all along."

Anthony Simcoe also considers the episode important for his character. "Even though they're warriors, Luxans are extremely spiritual," he explains, "and are really scared by anything magic or supernatural, because they believe in mysticism and magic. I really like showing that other side of the coin: 'What scares a Luxan?' Well, it's not a battle, it's not walking into impossible odds, or being surrounded by heaps of soldiers — it's a magician. It's someone who's going to mystically conjure up some otherworldliness." ■

Opposite page: Their spirits brought together by Maldis, Crichton confronts Crais.

Above: *Zhaan's psychic powers defeat Maldis.*

DNA MAD SCIENTIST

Written by: Tom Blomquist
Directed by: Andrew Prowse

Guest cast: Sarah Burns (Kornata), Adrian Getley (NamTar: movement), Julian Garner (NamTar: voice)

Crichton and the others visit the laboratory of NamTar, a bizarre, softly-spoken alien scientist, and his deformed assistant Kornata. The scientist's genetic database, compiled with information taken from extracted eye fluid, holds data covering eleven million species. NamTar may, therefore, be able to provide Moya's crew with genetic maps to their respective homeworlds, allowing them to plot courses which will avoid any Peacekeeper contact. His price? One of Pilot's four arms.

Despite Pilot's objections, D'Argo severs one of the shocked navigator's arms. Zhaan helps ease his pain while Rygel tells him to "think of someone else for a change." Crichton and Aeryn, appalled at D'Argo's barbarity, are not part of this bargain. Aeryn, an outcast, can never go home again and NamTar cannot find Earth among his galactic maps. While D'Argo, Zhaan and Rygel await NamTar's data crystal, arguing among themselves about whose homeworld Moya will be directed to first, Aeryn asks NamTar to find her an outlying Sebacean colony within the Uncharted Territories on which to settle. But has NamTar extracted a sample of her DNA, as he did with the others, or injected her with something dreadful?

Crichton to Aeryn

"When I find my way home - if I find my way home - I'll take you with me."

"Me, on a planet full of billions of you?"

Director Andrew Prowse recalls his feelings upon reading Rockne S. O'Bannon's draft of 'DNA Mad Scientist': "It had everything that drama needs in series television: characters with strong agendas, in conflict. I don't think we realised then that it was a turning point, but it solidified a lot of things. Once we'd shown that to the crew, we realised we could make strong, dramatic episodes — we could take off in a new direction."

"When I saw that script, I was horrified!" exclaims Virginia Hey, referring to the scene in which Zhaan helps amputate one of Pilot's arms. "Pilot was her friend, and she didn't even say she was sorry at the end! But they were adamant that I had to play it as it was." According to Matt Carroll, that action highlighted "the dysfunctionality of the group."

Hey remembers other aspects of the episode more fondly. "One amazing moment for me was seeing NamTar. Dave Elsey's just fantastic," she enthuses, referring to the creature effects supervisor who created the alien. But Adrian Getley, the man inside NamTar's suit, may not have felt the same way about the costume — at least initially. "Adrian spent two weeks on stilts, strapped into this costume," Hey recalls with a laugh. "We

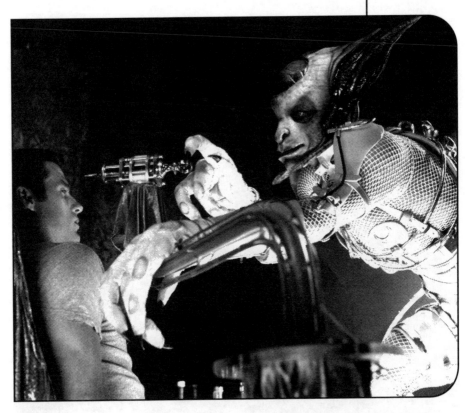

were all sweating because it was boiling, and I kept saying to Adrian, 'Drink water!' And he said, 'I can't. I can't go to the toilet; I have to wait until I'm out of the costume!' So I had a word in the costume designer's ear, and they got the scissors out and cut him a little escape hatch."

Terry Ryan, the man wielding the scissors on that occasion, recalls the thinking behind NamTar's bizarre appearance — part medical manual, part fetish magazine. "Because he's tricking around with people's DNA, he's sort of like a cosmetic surgeon who, when something worked on someone else, tried it on himself," he explains. "So we wanted his whole body to be held together by something from the outside. That's why we did the metal callipers and spine, and the hinges and bolts that came out and held his joints and body together." The idea, Ryan says, was that NamTar started out as a rat-like creature, "and kind of built himself up, hence the callipers on his legs. We also wanted to make him a bit androgynous, so we gave him a rounded breast, but also a full crotch, so you don't know where he's coming from!" Hey offers another secret of NamTar's design: "The animatronic head piece had Adrian's characteristics,"

Above: Crichton undergoes NamTar's procedure.

Next page: NamTar's genetic map shows Zhaan her home planet.

she laughs. "Adrian doesn't have mouse ears, but he has similar eyes, nose and mouth. It was like an exaggerated version."

According to David Kemper, the inspiration for the episode came from his first look at the finished, full-size Pilot prop: "We're standing there and I asked, 'Can we cut one of his arms off?' Matt Carroll was just stunned. He thought I was saying that the character should only have three arms, but I said, 'No, I want to cut one of his arms off in a story, but later he'll just regrow it, like a salamander can regrow its tail. What I want to know is, can you disconnect one of these arms, and then reattach it and everything's fine?' He said, 'Well, yeah...' And I said, 'That's all I need to know, thank you. By the way, he's great, I love him.' And I walked out of the room." Matt Carroll may have been a little bemused, but the seed had been sown for what was to become one of the biggest talking points of the first season. ■

| Written by: Sally Lapiduss | Guest cast: Alison Fox (Lo'Laan), Grant Magee (Jothee) |
| Directed by: Ian Watson | |

During maintenance work on Moya, to flush out the last elements of the Peacekeeper technology concealed within her infrastructure, D'Argo crawls into a service duct and locates a Peacekeeper device. Attempting to remove it, he triggers an explosive blast of particles, falls down a vertical shaft within Moya's propulsion system, and is ejected into space. D'Argo spends a quarter of an arn in the frozen void before he is brought back aboard the Leviathan, his Luxan physiology allowing him to survive — but just barely. In the depths of a "deep space interna-thermia" induced delirium, D'Argo believes that Zhaan is his dead wife, Lo'Laan, and Rygel his son, Jothee — family the others did not know he had. More alarmingly, Pilot begins to lose his symbiotic relationship with the Leviathan, the DRDs ambush Crichton and Aeryn, spraying them with an adhesive of some sort, and none of Moya's systems appear to be working properly. Could she have been infected by a virus left behind by the Peacekeepers and activated by the explosion, or is there something else going on?

Aeryn to Crichton

"You say that you want to go back to this place, Earth. A place that you tell me has so much disease and suffering."

"Well, you guys don't have chocolate."

In 'They've Got a Secret', the crew discover that they have inadvertently released the control to prevent the ship from becoming pregnant. Rockne S. O'Bannon recalls that at one point this revelation was going to come in the final scene of the opening episode. "In my very first version of the première script, written for the Fox network, the humorous 'button' of the episode was that the living ship has announced that she's pregnant. We decided to remove it from the end of the première, figuring it was too delicious a development to toss away at the end of an episode that already had a ton of stuff happening. So we held it in reserve, and as we began to develop the stories for the second half of the first year, where we started to fold in some multi-episode story arcs, we saw the opportunity to use it to its full advantage."

The storyline gave viewers an opportunity to investigate more of Moya's interior layout. "You'll notice that in the corridors, there's only one junction," notes production designer Ricky Eyres. "The corridor set breaks apart, and you've got ten different pieces which are all on wheels, so you can put them together in different layouts, like a child's construction set." Originally, Eyres explains, the corridor junctions would have functioned in three dimensions: "That's the one thing we didn't end up doing: an area that showed you going from level to level. In the original design, you could have climbed up the wall in the corridor, and at the junction you could have gone in six directions. It would be nice to go in that other dimension — up and down — which was on the original drawings, but we didn't achieve it."

There were other elements of Moya's design which were impossible to achieve, due to either time or budgetary constraints. "Originally, all the sets on Moya were going to be built on rostrums, off the deck, mainly to give us the facility to bring stuff through the floor," Eyres says. "As you walked into command, all the consoles were going to come up through the floor, for example. There was also talk of Moya having walkways that could move up and down, but to achieve that on our budget was not realistic and, I thought, fudged the logic of where certain things were in the ship." Overall, Eyres suggests, "we probably achieved about half of the

original ideas for Moya. But really, from a production design point of view, you aim for 150 per cent — and then you can normally achieve ninety."

Many of the regular actors found 'They've Got a Secret' one of the most rewarding of the first season episodes. "It was definitely one of my favourites," says Virginia Hey, "especially the scene where D'Argo was reminiscing about his wife and child. I found that very moving." Hey also has a more mischievous reason to remember the episode. "Another of my favourite moments was grabbing Crichton's crotch!" she says with a laugh. "I hadn't thought about it before now, but in retrospect, that was a lovely moment!"

One of a producer's responsibilities is to match directors to scripts — and Matt Carroll knew that Ian Watson was the perfect choice to direct a character-based episode. "I brought in Ian Watson because actors on long-running shows can get exhausted by action-oriented directors," says Carroll. "The other three directors," he adds, referring to series regulars Andrew Prowse, Tony Tilse and Rowan Woods, "are all very much action directors, and Ian is the performance director. So it meant that the actors get a chance to work with a director that's not going to be so driven by the action, and it worked very well." ■

Opposite page: The crew wonder why Moya's systems are malfunctioning.

Above: D'Argo remembers his wife and son.

Written by: Doug Heyes, Jr.	**Guest cast:** Magda Szubanski (Furlow), Jeremy Sims
Directed by: Tony Tilse	(Rorf), Jo Kerrigan (Rorg), Lani Tupu (Captain Bialar Crais)

Crichton and Aeryn are test-flying *Farscape 1*, refitted with some components from Moya, in an attempt to harness the mysterious properties produced by a solar flare — the same phenomenon which, Crichton believes, opened up the wormhole that brought him from Earth. Sure enough, history almost repeats itself: this time, *Farscape 1* escapes the wormhole, but springs a dangerous plasma leak. Moya resists efforts to bring the stricken ship aboard, evidently concerned for the well-being of her unborn child, and Crichton

Crichton to Rorf

"You help me capture the prisoners, and I'll split the bounty, seventy-thirty."

"Seventy-forty!"

is forced to land on a nearby desert world. Furlow, a mechanic Crichton finds at the Dam-Ba-Da depot, may be able to make repairs, but as Furlow begins work, the depot receives a holographic wanted beacon message from Captain Crais, alerting the locals to the identities of the fugitives D'Argo, Zhaan and Rygel (Crais wants to kill Crichton himself, and has other plans for Aeryn). This forces Crichton to strike a 'deal' with two Vorcarian Blood Trackers, Rorf and Rorg — bounty hunters with blood-red eyes — for the capture of the fugitives. As D'Argo travels down to the planet to pick up Crichton and Aeryn, leaving Zhaan to enjoy photogasms in the warmth of the sun, Crais offers Aeryn a deal of her own in a secret holograph: an honourable discharge in return for turning in Crichton and the rest of the crew...

'Till the Blood Runs Clear' was the second time that a wormhole effect was required. Unlike some visual effects, which can be reused, Paul Butterworth and his team had to develop the look almost from scratch again. "We took the internal, liquidy-tunnel idea from the première and developed it so we had a better entrance to the wormhole," he recalls. "It was nice to take it that much further and join the inside and the outside

ENCOUNTERS: VORCARIAN BLOOD TRACKERS

Beings with blood-red eyes, dog-like faces and a keen sense of smell — making them perfectly suited to the role of bounty hunter, which they adopt with enthusiasm. However, they have little in the way of intelligence (maths is a particular weak point), will submit to anyone they believe dominant, and can be led by their noses into giving up their prey.

better. It was sort of aqueous space. A lot of energy was spent on discussing what everything looked like — things were redesigned time and time again until everyone was happy."

The episode also features one of *Farscape*'s most striking locations, at Stockton Sands in Newcastle, two hours drive north of Sydney. "You look out one way to the Pacific, and you look back inland, and there's vegetation in the far distance," Pete Coogan recalls. "It was like the Sahara, with all these sand dunes. It was quite incredible, and we'd always wanted to shoot there. One of the biggest problems though was that the temperature was in the high nineties — not good for people in prosthetics!" Matt Carroll also remembers other problems filming in the desert brought. "It was probably the most difficult episode to execute," he agrees. "We had to take everything out into the middle of this sand desert in four wheel drives." Ricky Eyres remembers a particular shot that the location helped achieve: "There was a great exterior there, with the pull-down shot into the desert planet. That was a combination of how CG and sets work together. We did that big pull-down as Crichton and Aeryn walk through the door into what would be the exterior — a bit like the Mos Eisley spaceport in *Star Wars*."

Although actress Magda Szubanski, best known for her role in *Babe*,

Above: The Vorcarian Blood Trackers.

Next page: Crichton under fire at the Dam-Ba-Da depot.

makes quite an impression as Furlow (who was originally scripted as a
male character), the Vorcarian Blood Trackers, Rorf and Rorg, are equally
memorable. "I really liked the Blood Trackers," says costume designer
Terry Ryan. "We started off with that American western explorer sort of
style, and I thought of a costume with a lot of fringes, so that when they
walked everything swung and hung from their bodies. Their fringes were
made out of human hair, which worked a treat."

For Anthony Simcoe, the episode was a significant step in the development of D'Argo's relationship with Crichton. "There's a pivotal
moment in the relationship, where Crichton and D'Argo finally realise,
'Look, we may not be the best friends in the world, but we can be allies
and learn to get along.' We put a lot of effort into trying to make that
scene work, and I feel really happy with the results. It's also one of my
favourite 'goof reel' moments," he adds mischievously. "Crichton
explains that on Earth, men originally shook hands to show that they
weren't holding weapons, and D'Argo puts his weapon aside and shakes
Crichton's hand, and then 'Cut!' and we're out. But on the day, we carried on, said we loved each other and went into a big fake kiss!" ■

THE FLAX

Written by: Justin Monjo	Guest cast: Rhys Muldoon (Staanz), John Bachelor
Directed by: Peter Andrikidis	(Kcrackic), David Bowers (Goon)

oya, heavily pregnant, is now being pursued by bounty hunters as well as Peacekeepers. Outside the ship, Aeryn is teaching Crichton to fly a transport pod when suddenly it is pulled toward an invisible nexus floating in space, and becomes snagged like an insect in a spider's web. Meanwhile, an unarmed vessel requests permission to come aboard Moya. Its pilot is a Zenetan named Staanz, a former Peacekeeper prisoner who claims to be a "garbologist": a connoisseur of what other people throw away. Staanz tells D'Argo and Zhaan about the flax, an invisible 'drift net' placed by Zenetan pirates to snag unprepared ships. A distress call from the trapped transport pod seems to bear out his story, but D'Argo still mistrusts Staanz — especially when he notices that the Zenetan is wearing Luxan boots. Staanz explains that he found them while looting a Luxan ship, and offers to take D'Argo to it so that he can look for star maps that could help him find his way home. But as soon as they leave, Zhaan learns that Moya is about to be boarded by a gang of Zenetan pirates. In the transport pod, Aeryn and Crichton realise that they are going to have to depressurise in order to survive — and there is only one intact spacesuit...

Crichton to Aeryn

"Slicker'n snot."

"My microbes *had* to have translated that one wrongly."

While the concept of a web in space which ensnares ships was easy enough to understand, the visual-effects team had to work out a way to make it convincing on screen. "Originally, the flax was not going to be seen," Paul Butterworth recalls. "Basically, the ship would be falling through space and then just hit something and stop. There would be a bit of an energy burst, but you wouldn't see much. But that just doesn't make really good television. It wouldn't sell the concept."

The team came up with a solution that looked effective, but then other problems became apparent. "The ships had to appear to be stuck in

ENCOUNTERS: ZENETANS

Scavengers with exotic body markings and aggressive natures, many Zenetans are pirates by trade, attacking, boarding and looting ships which stray into their territory. In recent cycles, their piracy has been aided by their creation of the flax — described as "a magnadrift mesh seventy-five million zacrons long" — in which their victims can easily become trapped.

space," Butterworth says, "but it's really hard to show a ship just sitting there, and then have the camera move around it with interesting angles, without it looking like it's moving. Then there were other shots where we had to have a ship moving away from us, or moving around, but because there was no relationship to the space around it, it caused lots of problems. You couldn't work out whether the ship was moving or just standing there!"

"The shuttle that you see caught in the web is a combination of CG and a standing set, which has been used in several episodes," explains Ricky Eyres, who designed the spacecraft. "It's a really interesting ship, if I say so myself! It's kind of like a truck and trailer, in that what they're flying around is the basic unit, and you can add on pieces to the back, like Moya containers, so the thing could actually be ten miles long. These extra bits and pieces kind of lock on the back — there was a whole drawing

done of the mechanics of how that worked. I suppose it's a bit like *Thunderbird 2*," he considers, referring to the multi-purpose rescue craft from the Gerry Anderson puppet show *Thunderbirds*, "but cooler!"

Another CG/standing set combination appearing in this episode was originally designed to become a regular feature of Moya. "There's a point on Moya which is a bubble dome, where Crichton and Aeryn go to talk at the end of the episode," Matt Carroll explains. "It's a huge green screen shot, showing this transparent bubble where they're looking out into space. We built it as a set which we thought we'd be able to re-use very easily. But it was an expensive shot to do, and the dome didn't really work for anything other than having an intimate moment; it wasn't a location on board the ship that drove other stories — so we ended up just using it once."

For Claudia Black, 'The Flax' showed the crew's commitment to each other becoming more important than their desire to go home: "As the season progresses, choices regarding whether or not they will be able to go home become progressively harder to make. In 'The Flax', D'Argo oscillates between, 'Do I go home to find my son, or do I save Crichton and Aeryn?' And he makes a choice that pleases Aeryn a lot." ■

*Opposite page:
Moya's transport pod
is caught in the flax.*

*Above: Rygel
challenges the
Zenetan pirate
Kcrackic to a game
of Tadek.*

Teleplay by: David Kemper	Guest cast: Darlene Vogel (Alex/Lorana), Kate Raison
Story by: David Kemper and Ro Hume	(Pa'u Tahleen), Max Phipps (Pa'u Tuzak), Michael Beckley (Hasko), Aaron Cash (Pa'u Bitaal), Grant Magee (Jothee),
Directed by: Andrew Prowse	Robert Supple (Young Crichton)

Crichton has a vivid dream about his former girlfriend, Alex. He wakes to find Moya in mid-StarBurst, apparently in response to the distress call of another pregnant Leviathan. Crichton soon learns that the others also have had dreams that evoke strong emotions. It appears that Moya's emotional responses were triggered by Pa'u Tahleen, leader of a small colony of Delvian missionaries who broke away from a corrupt Delvian regime and now make their home on a remote, toxic planetoid they have dubbed "The New Moon of Delvia." Tahleen attempts to convince Zhaan to join the uprising, engage with her in the sacred ceremony of Unity — the bonding of two minds and two souls — and follow their spiritual leader, Pa'u Tuzak. But Tuzak is beginning to succumb to the dark impulses to which all Delvians are vulnerable — even Zhaan. Tahleen shows Zhaan what she is capable of — she makes Crichton believe that Alex has joined him on his *Farscape* mission, and convinces D'Argo that his son Jothee is aboard Moya. When Zhaan reluctantly agrees to Unity with Tahleen, she discovers that her calming abilities are not what the leader seeks — and dark powers within Zhaan begin to hold sway once more...

> **D'Argo to Rygel**
>
> "I sense Delvian trickery here, Rygel. We must leave this place."
>
> "Get the food first."

It's no surprise that Virginia Hey considers 'Rhapsody in Blue' her favourite *Farscape* story. "That whole episode was very important for me, and I learned a great deal," says Hey, who found the background of her character expanding rapidly within the course of a single script. "Andrew Prowse directed that episode, and I loved every second of it. He really pushed my performance, and I think that since then, there's been a great strength in Zhaan that was borne out of that particular story. As an actor, I found another dimension to her. It's not necessarily obvious on screen, but was obvious to me inside. Now Zhaan's more complicated, and has more depth.

"Each week, I get new scripts which give me the progress of Zhaan's life, and it's like getting a Christmas present every week," Hey reveals. So, receiving the script for 'Rhapsody in Blue', focusing on the Delvians in general and on Zhaan in particular, must have been like Christmas and her birthday rolled into one. "I was in heaven," she agrees, "but when we

started shooting, I also felt like I was in some kind of strange bowling alley in the sky. We had a big laugh behind the scenes, because the Delvian girls had hair that reminded us of those elderly ladies who dye their hair purple or blue, and want to go bowling!" And the other Delvian women actually had hair! "I was laughing about that too, and saying, 'Okay, so tell me, if all Delvian women have hair, and all Delvian men are bald, then what the hell am I? Drag queen incarnate? I know I'm masculine, but this is ridiculous!'"

Director Andrew Prowse recalls the thinking behind the episode. "The problem with saints is that they're fundamentally excruciatingly boring," he jokes, "and you want them to have internal conflicts." Zhaan had been set up as saintly and philosophical, but suddenly here was a surprising new aspect to her character. "Rather than gradually change her into something else, we decided to do it with an axe!" Prowse says. "It shocked a lot of people: learning that Zhaan had killed her lover, and was part of a culture that wanted to destroy things. We were throwing preconceptions up against the wall and breaking them."

According to Paul Butterworth, the joining of minds, or Unity between Crichton and Zhaan was a prime example of creating a very effective

Above: Zhaan enters into Unity with Tahleen.

Next page: Crichton joined with Zhaan in Unity.

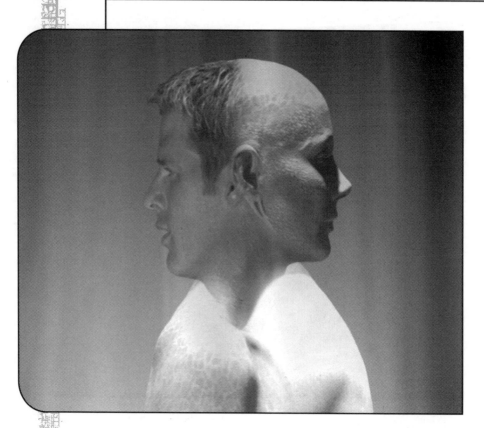

visual sequence whilst under pressure. "The fusion thing came about as a last minute thought while we were on set," he recalls. The script called for an effect where the audience would see Unity as two hands, one inside the other. "That effect was going to be made prosthetically," Butterworth continues, "but I think in the end the shot was dropped from the script. So we came up with this stylistic idea, looking at it from a side-on point of view. What I wanted to do originally was show it with a motion control shot, and circle around them, so you had a two-faced head of Janus, seeing Zhaan and then Crichton." While this exact effect wasn't possible to achieve in the time available, the depiction of Unity in the finished episode was nevertheless very effective.

Rockne S. O'Bannon notes that a side issue revealed in 'Rhapsody in Blue' is the insidious effect of the Peacekeepers — once you invite them in, it's hard to get rid of them: "The Delvians hired the Peacekeepers to not necessarily keep law and order among themselves, because that wasn't really needed, but to protect them from outside — and that was a big mistake!" ∎

JEREMIAH CRICHTON

Written by: Doug Heyes, Jr.	Guest cast: Natalie Mendoza (Lishala), Kevin Copeland
Directed by: Ian Watson	(Rokon), John O'Brien (Kato-Re), Deni Gordon (Neera),
	Tania Mustapic (Maid)

Finding it increasingly frustrating to make himself and his human 'foibles' understood, Crichton decides to take *Farscape 1* out for a spin. But no sooner has his module left Moya, than the pregnant Leviathan compensates for a severe pressure build-up in her amnexus system by initiating a sudden StarBurst, unintentionally leaving Crichton stranded in space. Crichton winds up on Acquara, an Earth-like world, where he has been welcomed. He also has been befriended by the beautiful Lishala, daughter of the Acquaran ruler — which has aroused the jealousy of Rokon, a rival for Lishala's affections. A quarter of a cycle later, still arguing over the relative merits of their rescue mission, D'Argo and Rygel arrive on Acquara by transport pod, but technical difficulties soon arise: communication with Moya is severed, and both the pod and D'Argo's weapon have gone dead. Could something on the surface be draining power? And if so, how will Crichton, D'Argo, and Rygel rejoin the others on Moya?

Crichton

"Since I left my home, I've been hunted, beaten, locked up, shanghaied, shot at... I've had alien creatures in my face, up my nose, inside my brain, down my pants... This is the first time, the first place, where I've found peace."

The inspiration for 'Jeremiah Crichton' came from an unexpected source. "I was having dinner at Ben Browder's house," David Kemper recalls, "and his wife says to me, 'Ben's favourite movie is *Jeremiah Johnson*, a Robert Redford movie from 1972. It's about a man who goes native with the Indians, lives up in the mountains, and forsakes society.' Instantly I had an idea for doing 'Jeremiah Crichton' — Crichton goes native, lives among the people and grows a beard. The next morning I had the story in my head, and I called Rockne and told

ENCOUNTERS: ACQUARANS

Inhabitants of the Earth-like world of Acquara, a planet where, although only males of the species can rule, females choose their own mates. Thus, whoever the daughter of the Grondeer (leader) marries, will rule Acquara after the Grondeer's death. The Acquarans' ancestors were Hynerian-ruled colonists, exiled to the planet and abandoned by one of Rygel's predecessors, Rygel X. For countless cycles, the Acquarans have awaited the return of their legendary saviour, fabled — according to their sacred text, the Timbala — to one day "rise up, and lead them into the light."

him. The aim was to get off the ship, and so we went down to a planet."

The clothing of the episode's Acquaran tribe saw costume designer Terry Ryan in especially fine form. "Terry uses some great colours," enthuses production designer Ricky Eyres. "I like bold colours, and I had spoken to Terry a lot about the tribes I had seen while I was doing *The Young Indiana Jones Chronicles* in Kenya. When you see Earth colours, like umbers and sand colours, with bright, vibrant turquoise or purple colours in front, it's just stunning. I'd seen that in Africa; colours that had come from the earth, because that's how those tribes make their colours up. And Terry's outrageous like that — not only can he put colours together, but he really knows how to make the finished costume work!"

The tribal nature of the Acquarans also inspired composer Chris Neal. "That episode required an almost Polynesian feel," he says. "It's an interesting thing, because you can have a slight influence, but you just can't go there too closely, because then it sounds Polynesian, and you lose the idea that it's an alien world. So you just get a sniff of an influence in there, and then bring that into our standard *Farscape* themes — which, in any case, are not so much themes as sound styles."

Pete Coogan remembers that the filming of 'Jeremiah Crichton' was quite

literally hit with problems — a calamitous hailstorm threatened to destroy the sets. "Hailstones the size of cricket balls came down," he recalls. "They came through the Creature Shop roof and through the production office windows. It was amazing!"

Opposite page:
Crichton is marooned
on Acquara.

The scenes with Rygel flying around on Acquara on his ThroneSled initially caused concern. Series creator O'Bannon recalls: "A new writer had come in, and he had Rygel rolling down a hill. And we said, 'It's going to be like three guys — the puppeteers — rolling down with him. How exactly do we manage this?'" Accordingly, the episode marked the longest appearance of the computer generated version of Rygel.

Above: Lishala and
her suitor Rokon.

"One great attribute of this episode is its glimpse into Rygel's world back home," O'Bannon adds. "The writers work very hard to keep Rygel a real character, not a puppet who's only there to pop off a few funny lines. In this story we saw Rygel learn that his minions back home were capable of performing some pretty despicable acts in his name. Although this was going on right under his nose while he was on Hyneria, he never noticed it, or chose not to notice it. Only with his present perspective — having lived over 100 cycles as a common prisoner and fugitive — has he gained the insight to truly see the evil of his minions' actions." ■

DURKA RETURNS

| Written by: Grant McAloon | Introducing: Gigi Edgley (Chiana) |
| Directed by: Tony Tilse | Guest cast: David Wheeler (Captain Selto Durka), Tiriel Mora (Salis) |

oya's ability to StarBurst is severely affected by her pregnancy. Emerging from her latest attempt, she collides with a Nebari transport ship, damaging it in the process. The stricken ship is brought aboard Moya with its three occupants: Salis, a Nebari official; Chiana, the beautiful Nebari criminal in his custody; and a Sebacean who bears a striking resemblance to the infamous Peacekeeper Durka. The Sebacean admits that he is, indeed, Durka, but Salis assures the crew that Durka's aggressive impulses have been removed through a kind of Nebari 'mind control'. Crichton is disturbed by this technique, particularly when he meets Chiana, whose only crime, she claims, is wanting to get away from the "half-dead sanctimoniousness of my planet." Rygel, meanwhile, is set on revenge against his torturer, while Aeryn is somewhat awed by Durka — until she learns that he dishonoured her people by faking his death and deserting the *Zelbinion*. But Durka does appear to be a reformed man — until Rygel tries to assassinate him...

> **Crichton to Chiana**
>
> "We have rules."
>
> "Yeah. Well when I see any of you following them, so will I."

"Durka was supposed to be a Peacekeeper villain from 200 years or so before, so we made him slightly Napoleonic," costume designer Terry Ryan says of the infamous character. "At the beginning, when he's under the influence of the Nebari, he's sort of dressed like them, but later on he shows his true colours, so to speak."

"That episode was my favourite — totally, hands down," says Gigi Edgley of her *Farscape* début. "I think it's my favourite probably because I was the most frightened, and the most challenged, and the most excited. Chiana's character had a really big impact on me, and I could really play around with her, as she was sussing out this new ship. And that was

ENCOUNTERS: NEBARI

A vastly powerful race, the Nebari are responsible for the conquering of the legendary Peacekeeper ship the *Zelbinion*. They have white skin and deep black eyes, and are native to Nebari Prime. They quell all forms of rebellion and dissent among their people by placing non-conformist citizens in control collars, and forcibly removing their rebellious tendencies through a supposedly irreversible corrective mind control process known as 'mental cleansing'.

completely real: the ship actually *was* new to me, because it was basically only the second time I'd ever come onto the Leviathan set. Plus I was wearing the contact lenses which give me total tunnel vision — very alienating! And then seeing this all-American chunk of hunk come up to me, I just go, 'Hmm, what can we play here?'"

That all-American 'chunk of hunk' — Ben Browder — also enjoyed the episode. "There's a terrific explosion in 'Durka Returns', when Rygel rolls the bomb in the bay, and they set off an explosion right behind me," recalls Browder. "I fell into frame; we were on a twenty second delay and it was a wide angle. I was totally obscured by the flame and of course I was smoking from my backside! I fell over and then immediately popped back up, and we got a kind of production value that you don't usually get on television. It was worth it because it looked fantastic. I guess you could do it digitally," he adds, "but you don't get the same reaction. You don't get that real John Crichton look of fear!"

Paul Butterworth recalls another difficult visual effect: "'Durka Returns' has one of the trickiest shots that we did — marrying a live-action actor running up a drawbridge into the spaceship, with the camera swinging

Above: The return of the infamous Peacekeeper.

Next page: The Nebari transport ship attempts to leave Moya.

around a large 3D matte painting and looking inside the window to see him fire up the spaceship." So, how was it done? "We shot a locked-off camera of Durka running into the maintenance bay, running up just a flat panel of wood, and then filmed a little element of Durka in the spaceship at the control desk. Then we composited those two elements within the actual scene of the CG matte painting itself."

Although there is very little to laugh about in the tension-filled 'Durka Returns', one joke was obvious to members of the crew, if not the audience: the physical appearance of Salis was based on director of photography Craig Barden. "Craig is a bit of an Elvis — a fifties rock and roller," make-up supervisor Lesley Vanderwalt laughs. "We were all teasing him, and when I had done Gigi's make-up and decided what she was going to look like, we decided that Salis should look similar. We did a test and played with him, putting sideburns on like Craig's. The wig for the character had thick black hair material, so we did the old Elvis quiff — and ended up with a black and white version of Craig!" ■

A HUMAN REACTION

Written by: Justin Monjo **Directed by:** Rowan Woods	**Guest cast:** Kent McCord (Jack Crichton), Phillip Gordon (Ray Wilson), Richard Sydenham (Cobb), Frankie Davidson (Newsstand Guy), Albert Mensah (Dialectic), Andy Cachia (Technician), Selina Muller (Woman on Beach)

ilot alerts Crichton to the existence of a wormhole, almost identical to the one which brought him from Earth, but cautions that it is rapidly growing unstable. Crichton catches a glimpse of a familiar-looking blue planet on the far side. Could it be home? Despite the dangers of the wormhole's instability, Crichton powers up *Farscape 1* and asks Aeryn to accompany him. Fearing that she will not fit in on his world, she declines and they bid each other farewell. Crichton heads for the wormhole, emerges on the other side, and makes a crash-landing on the Australian shoreline. Expecting a warm welcome, he is instead shot with a tranquiliser dart, closely examined and interrogated relentlessly by the military. With alien microbes in his brain and *Farscape 1* fitted out with extra-terrestrial technology, Crichton is treated with extreme suspicion, despite his father's assurances that he is, indeed, his son. But when Aeryn, D'Argo and Rygel follow Crichton through the wormhole and land on Earth, John's loyalties are sorely tested...

> **Rygel to Crichton**
>
> "It's just a tiny blue planet, what are you getting worked up about? It's got no particle rings, no red moons..."
>
> "That's Earth. That's my home."

With echoes of both *The Truman Show* and 'The Chimes of Big Ben' (an episode of sixties television series *The Prisoner* in which Patrick McGoohan's Number 6 thinks he has returned home, only to find that he has been cheated), 'A Human Reaction' stands as one of the series' high points. The audience is kept guessing about what's happening until the final few minutes, and the performances Rowan Woods encourages from the cast are among the finest of the first season.

"I absolutely adored that episode," says Ben Browder. "The characters remain the same, all the rules are the same, but the fact that it's taking place

ENCOUNTERS: THE ANCIENTS

A strange race with the ability to manipulate matter into the patterns of other beings' memories, the Ancients have wormhole technology and are able to implant information deep within the unconscious mind of other life forms. They have been searching for a new home and use Crichton's memories to find out how humans would react to alien creatures.

on 'Earth' changes the whole tone of the acting. It's got a quieter, more lyrical quality to it, and yet a dark and *X-Files* kind of edge about it. It's just fantastic." The story has a significant moment for Aeryn — her first experience of rain — a touch which wasn't in the original script. "It was supposed to be a beautiful sunny day," Browder recalls. "We were going to look at this beautiful sunset, but then the location got hit with rain, so the whole tenure of the piece shifted. Aeryn has spent her entire life on ships. She has barely been onto a planet. That's something that Claudia knew and the writers had instilled, but was never thoroughly demonstrated until we had that rain, and Claudia latches on and goes, 'Rain. Is that what you call this? I like it.' And Rowan Woods is a master of taking that moment and then informing the whole piece with it."

Dave Elsey was equally satisfied with the episode, especially the Creature Shop's realisation of the Ancients. "They were huge," he says. "The great big pod things were each about nine feet long. The set was just a big concrete bunker, so the three creatures *were* the set, really. The heads were silicone, and full of lights, which you could see playing around under the skin." As for the creatures' remarkable eyes, Elsey reveals that they were inspired by the 'plasma ball' lights found in many homes and offices. "One

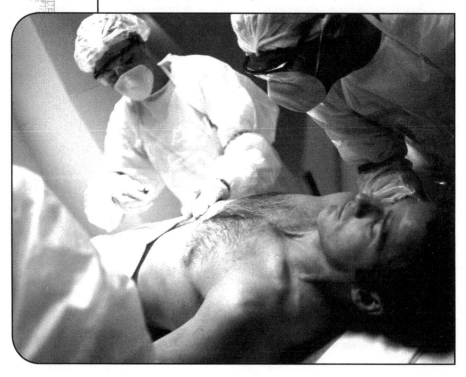

of my guys had one of those things, and we were just playing around with it while we were talking about how to do the eyes of the Ancients. And I just said, 'Hang on, what about one of these?' So we bought a whole bunch of them, and they looked fantastic." Another of Elsey's remarkable creations was what he calls the 'drone' alien. "What you see there is a rod puppet that was being puppeteered by several people standing against green screens, rather like C-3PO in *Star Wars Episode One*," he reveals. "Then they digitally remove the puppeteers, and suddenly you've got a really weird-looking 'stick insect' creature that's moving around right in front of Crichton."

Opposite page: Crichton undergoes a battery of tests.

Above: *Crichton learns the truth about his experiences on 'Earth'.*

"That was a really big music episode, because of the journey that we were asking the audience to take," composer Chris Neal explains. "For *Farscape 1* landing on the beach at the beginning, we went very conventional, but as we followed Crichton's growing realisation that something was terribly wrong, the music had to become progressively weirder, until we get to the exposure of who his father really is. The music really goes hell for leather at that point." Neal particularly liked the truth behind Rygel's autopsy, as revealed at the climax: "That was a great idea — far from being gutted, Rygel's actually *filling* his guts, with those wonderful Hynerian snails he's eating!" ∎

Written by: David Kemper	Regular cast only
Directed by: Ian Watson	

The crew are arguing about the wisdom of remaining aboard Moya, fearing the effects of her pregnancy may eventually cause them to be recaptured by the Peacekeepers. Overhearing the conversation, and sympathising with their concerns, Moya attempts to StarBurst — unwise, given that she does not have the energy to do so. As she comes to a dead stop, having apparently collided with something in mid-StarBurst, D'Argo, Aeryn and Rygel disappear in flashes of vivid colours. Pilot reports that they are all still on board, but no trace of them can be found. Crichton is searching the ship when he is swallowed up in a burst of brilliant red, still on board the Leviathan, but in the midst of all manner of strange phenomena. Sound, colour, light and balance are all affected — almost as if the Leviathan and everything on it is shifting in and out of different dimensions. Crichton discovers each of the crewmembers on a separate dimensional 'level' of Moya. When a gigantic claw begins cutting its way through the ship, the crew realise that to escape they are going to need Pilot on every 'level' — or become trapped between dimensions.

Crichton to Chiana

"Listen, sunshine, do you wanna be part of this crew?"

"On your good days."

"This is one of the good days."

'Through the Looking Glass' went through many permutations before arriving on the screen. Years ago David Kemper had pitched it as a potential storyline for *Star Trek: The Next Generation*. *Farscape* creator Rockne S. O'Bannon recalls, "the *Enterprise* comes across a ship that seems to be derelict. Their people go on board and the ship is empty, but the walls have this kind of slime on them, which they discover is actually a creature like a hermit crab, which takes over the ship and lives within it. When it gets larger, it has to find a bigger home, so now it heads for the *Enterprise*."

ENCOUNTERS: TRANS-DIMENSIONAL ENTITY

Trans-dimensional entities of unknown origin, possibly comprised of anti-matter, which exist in an unknown dimension, incompatible with our own. Although their manifestation can be extremely alarming to species who exist in only three dimensions, the trans-dimensional entities act to repair breaches between dimensions, or 'dimensional schisms', and also possess the ability to communicate with other species instantaneously.

The core of this idea was subsequently transferred to *Farscape*. Matt Carroll recalls early discussions about "a nasty sort of green slime thing that got on board and was eating away at things. We didn't want to waste any ideas," he adds, "but that was certainly one where the original concept was vastly changed." The new version — with Moya trapped mid-StarBurst, multiple dimensions, and a strange creature leaving claw marks in mid-air — became an episode for the latter part of the season because of the lengthy time involved in conceptualising it.

"It was the hardest episode for everyone to grasp," Paul Butterworth recalls. "David Kemper had this idea that a piece of paper is a flat, 2D plane which projects a 3D shadow. Well, he must have been imagining this beast, whatever it was, projecting out a *five* dimensional shadow or something, but no one had an idea of what this inter-dimensional creature looked like, and David didn't really want the audience to see it. So, conceptually, it was one of those things that was bounced around for a long time before we came up with what we had, which was the claw tearing through. But you didn't really get to see the claw either — the tears just

Above: Moya is trapped between dimensions.

Next page: Facing the trans-dimensional entity.

opened up into white space. It was on the other side of whatever that reality is, that you got to see the creature, with its tentacles floating around."

The unique colour scheme of 'Through the Looking Glass' gave the music and sound departments plenty to consider. "We actually had to work really closely with the sound department, because there were the yellow, the red and the blue dimensions," composer Chris Neal explains. "So, for example, musically, we kind of stayed out of the yellow dimension — the 'happy' dimension — and left it to the sound people, and concentrated on the music for the red and the blue dimensions. With the red one, we used a lot of bottom end to give it a lot of threat, and then in the blue level, it was a dreamier kind of approach."

Gigi Edgley notes that the episode developed the relationship between Chiana and Rygel a little further. "Ryge and Chiana hang out with each other for a purpose," she considers. "They would still sell the other one out, but I think they know they make a good team, because they're probably the two most disloyal ones on the ship!" ∎

A BUG'S LIFE

Story by: Doug Heyes, Jr. **Teleplay by:** Stephen Rae **Directed by:** Tony Tilse	**Guest cast:** Paul Leyden (Captain Larraq), Richard White (Thorrn), Zoe Coyle (Science Officer Hassan), Michael Tuahine (Rhed)

As a platoon of 'special ops' Peacekeepers — known as Black Ghosts — board Moya in their crippled Marauder, the Leviathan's crew attempt a daring bluff: Crichton and Aeryn pretend to be Peacekeepers in charge of the ship, with Chiana as their server, while D'Argo, Zhaan and Rygel assume the role of prisoners. The plan begins to unravel when Captain Larraq, citing Article 414-Decca of the Peacekeepers' Code, assumes command of the ship to complete his Priority Red One mission — the delivery of a package to a secret Gammak base run by the Peacekeeper Science Military, in the Uncharted Territories just twenty arns away. Chiana and Rygel, both snooping around the Peacekeepers' cargo, agree to share anything of value they find. Managing to open a locked container, they discover a strange species, lying in suspended animation. Disturbed by Rhed, one of the Peacekeepers, they hide, but watch as he makes contact with the sleeping creature, apparently becoming infected by it. Larraq explains that the captured alien was carrying a deadly virus, which can only infect one host at a time — providing it doesn't get the chance to stay inside one life form long enough to lay a couple of million spores. When Rygel disappears, everyone assumes that the virus has infected him — unaware that he wasn't the only one who was exposed...

> ### Rygel to Chiana
>
> "How dare you sneak up on me like that! I should make you wear a bell 'round your neck!"
>
> "Keep your fantasies to yourself, frog boy."

"That was just a good sort of shoot-'em-up episode, really," says Paul Butterworth, adding that the special visual-effects were principally "just different types of laser rifle fire." The script did present the opportunity for the visual effects department to achieve something that they had wanted to try in 'Exodus from Genesis' — combining a lot of live-action footage

ENCOUNTERS: INTELLANT VIRUS

An invisible virus which infects virtually any life form through physical contact. Using the species as a host, the virus lays millions of spores. While it inhabits the host, there is no way of detecting the virus. When it exits, it leaves behind a mild hallucinogenic, disorienting the victim. However, a victim's acidity levels are increased — meaning that those who were infected can be identified.

with computer generated, 3D imagery of a Peacekeeper Marauder. However, the team was unable to shoot one particular scene — one showing the Peacekeepers running down the ship's gangplank — since it proved impossible to have the gangplank built in time. "We had them all jump down on wires," Butterworth explains, "and then we stripped that into the shot instead."

The episode also sees D'Argo, Zhaan and Rygel return to their cells, while Crichton and Aeryn carry out their subterfuge. The cells always had a dual purpose in production designer Ricky Eyres's mind: originally storage areas, they would have been altered to suit their new role when the Peacekeepers turned Moya into a prison ship. "They were really like a hive, although we never established that," he says. "We should have done a shot showing there were thirty of them on either side of the corridor, and also on other levels. The thing about those shots is that you can reuse them every now and again, and each time you drop them in, it just reinforces the scale of Moya. There's a functional idea there too, about the way the ship would be loaded, and the way she would store materials."

David Kemper recalls being impressed by Gigi Edgley's performance, as she settled into her role. "It's hard to find a twenty year-old girl

who's an accomplished actress," he points out. "You can find really pretty twenty year-old girls, or you can find really accomplished actresses who are thirty, but it's hard to find a twenty-year-old that can get us the shots, and step into an ensemble that's essentially stage trained. You bring in a twenty year-old and you expect her to be scared. Gigi was, to a degree, but she stood right in there and she gave it to them!"

Ben Browder's ability to ad lib dialogue on set is greatly valued by the cast and production team, and Claudia Black enjoys watching him "work his way through various pop culture references until he finds exactly the right one." O'Bannon is unabashedly in awe of Browder's abilities in this respect, and recalls that, in the scene where Crichton is trying to comprehend the scope of the intellant virus, Browder came up with a line which added immeasurably to the script: "Ben says, 'You might think your magic pill worked, and then Rygel's up walking around the ship, coughing up the spores, cats and dogs living together...' It's a line from *Ghostbusters*, and he delivers it exactly the way Bill Murray did. The minute I heard this ad libbing, I went, 'That's fantastic!' I would never in a million years have had the guts to put it in, even if it had occurred to me, because I would have thought it too much of an inside joke!" ■

Opposite page: Captain Larraq discovers the first victim of the intellant virus.

Above: Using Larraq as its host, the virus defends itself.

Written by: Richard Manning Directed by: Rowan Woods	Guest cast: Lani Tupu (Captain Bialar Crais), Wayne Pygram (Scorpius), Alyssa-Jane Cook (Gilina Mays), Paul Goddard (Stark), Imogen Annesley (Niem), Stephen Leeder (Commander Javio), Anthony Kierann (Lt Heskon), Christian Bischoff (Bixx), Pete Walters (Crais's Guard)

nable to regain full strength after being stabbed by the virus-infected Captain Larraq, Aeryn realises that her paraphoral nerve has been damaged, and unless she has a tissue graft from a genetically compatible donor, she will be dead within fifty or sixty arns. In the hopes of finding a suitable genetic donor, Crichton will attempt to infiltrate the Gammak base. While the others see the mission as suicidal, Chiana insists upon accompanying him. Crichton manages to bluff his way through base security — thanks to a maximum clearance identity chip Chiana stole from Larraq. When stopped at a security cordon to scan his DNA, he 'passes' the test thanks to the intervention of Gilina Mays, the Peacekeeper tech he and the others rescued from the *Zelbinion*. She offers to synthesise a tissue sample for Aeryn, who is quickly deteriorating. Crichton is about to leave with the sample when he is discovered by Scorpius — the Scarran half-breed in charge of the Gammak base. Chiana makes it back to Moya with the graft, but Scorpius has strapped Crichton in the Aurora Chair, a torture device used to extract memories. Crichton will either tell Scorpius everything he knows or die in the process...

Scorpius to Crichton

"Allow us to probe freely, for any information we wish..."

"Fetch the comfy chair."

"I think that 'Nerve' is actually the calling card for the show," states Ben Browder. "You're not changing the rules, and you're not trying to fool the audience. You're not changing the show for the sake of change, it's just that the story leads you to a certain place and it's going to evolve from there."

Indeed, 'Nerve' was a significant episode for a variety of reasons: not only did it kick off the first *Farscape* two-part story — ending, in time-honoured fashion, with the words 'To be continued' — but it also introduced Scorpius. Although Scorpius's prosthetic make-up played a major part in defining his personality, his costume was equally important. "With someone called Scorpius, you immediately think he's got to be like an insect, walking around with this hard black shell," Terry Ryan explains, recalling the earliest, overtly insectoid designs for the character. "If they had gone for an actor who was five foot two and eighteen stone, you would have gone a different way with him, but he's 'cool' evil, not 'melodramatic villain' evil — his power is very low-key, the way he uses it. We also

wanted him to be encased in a costume that was all strapped up, and looked like it was holding him together, so people might say, 'Why is he wearing that mask? Is it because his face might fall apart?'" Virginia Hey can remember the first time she saw Scorpius on set. "I was floored by this futuristic S&M post-punk pop star in his alligator suit!"

Chris Neal had no trouble giving Scorpius his own signature theme music. "With 'Scorpie'," Neal says, using the *Farscape* crew's nickname for the Scarran-Sebacean half-breed, "we always had a very dark, processed male choir sort of moaning sound, which we used most of the time he was on screen. And in that episode where we first meet him, we started introducing a different line of militaristic Peacekeeper music, so you get some snares and drum rolls coming in there."

"I love the scenes between D'Argo and Aeryn," says Anthony Simcoe, referring to his character's refusal to abandon the ailing Sebacean, even though he has promised to allow her to die alone. "It's a real warrior code sort of thing, a mutual respect between these two people

Above: Scorpius tortures Crichton in the Aurora Chair.

Next page: Scorpius continues his ruthless procedure.

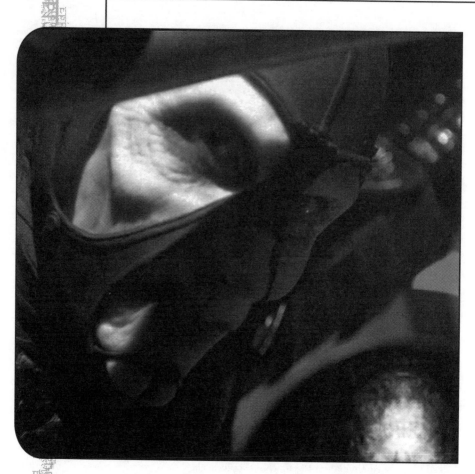

who've really gone hammer-and-tongs at each other for the whole season. You really can see the respect, and it's a beautiful sign of the journey that the characters have made. When he says, 'I'll stay here, and watch over her,' to be there while she's recovering — it's really a lovely moment." Claudia Black agrees. "We see D'Argo's growing respect and affection for her when her paraphoral nerve is punctured," she says. "He makes specific choices to protect and save her despite her willingness to embrace death."

'Nerve' created an unusual problem for the make-up department, as Chiana is forced to wear a Sebacean disguise in place of her own distinctive hair and skin colouring. "I was saying, 'Where did she get that boot polish for her hair? How did that happen?'" laughs Gigi Edgley. "I was a bit nervous, because I thought it was a bit early on to give away what Gigi looks like underneath Chiana's make-up, but they said, 'Don't worry, she's not going to look like you — she's going to look like Chiana in disguise!'" ■

THE HIDDEN MEMORY

Written by: Justin Monjo Directed by: Ian Watson	Guest cast: Lani Tupu (Captain Bialar Crais), Wayne Pygram (Scorpius), Alyssa-Jane Cook (Gilina Mays), Paul Goddard (Stark), Imogen Annesley (Niem), Anthony Kierann (Lt Heskon), Christian Bischoff (Bixx), Pete Walters (Crais's Guard), Nicole Roma (Blonde Technician)

ith Crichton being tortured on the Gammak base by Scorpius and Crais, and Aeryn still recovering from her tissue transplant, Moya goes into labour. Learning of Crichton's plight, Aeryn insists on trying to rescue him, and is accompanied to the base by D'Argo and Zhaan. During a session in the Aurora Chair, Crichton reveals memories of a meeting with Crais, in which he gave Crais information on wormholes. But Crichton and Crais never had such a conversation — Gilina has programmed the false memories into the Chair so Crichton can tell Scorpius what he wants to hear. Scorpius now is sure Crais is keeping other information from him — and orders that Crais be put in the Chair. Aeryn rescues Crichton and Stark, his half-mad cellmate, but with Moya encountering complications during the birthing process, they cannot be certain they have a ship to return to — if they even succeed in escaping from the Gammak base...

Scorpius to Crichton

"I know you're living on a stolen Leviathan with escaped prisoners, and I know that Leviathan is pregnant."

"You know who the daddy is?"

Both the cast and crew recall the atmosphere on the set of 'The Hidden Memory' as electric, with the Aurora Chair scenes being particularly powerful. Pete Coogan remembers a moment between Ben Browder and Lani Tupu: "It was when Crichton's in the chair and Crais is torturing him," he explains. "The close-up is Crais almost spitting in Crichton's face and Lani's really going for it. Ben's terrific, and there's blood on his face. It's coming to the end and it looks as if Crichton's going to die... and when the director shouted, 'Cut!', Lani put his hand on Ben's shoulder — he was actually really concerned for him. Then, as soon as the call for action came, *bang*, he was Crais again."

Claudia Black remembers another moment from the Aurora Chair sequences. "Lani and I came to our scene," she recalls, "where I told Crais I'd show him his life. There was one revolution of the chair, and Lani was screaming — and we lost power! The entire unit shut down. We lost light, the chair stopped, and there's Crais in the chair. It was just a classic moment — a bloodcurdling scream and the power stopped."

The shots showing the approach to the Gammak base allowed Paul Butterworth to try out some new visual techniques: "The base itself was a large matte painting, projected onto 3D geometry so you could actually do flyovers of it. So, essentially, rather than build everything in a detailed 3D form, we could get away with a painting." The scenes with the Aurora Chair involved a lot of 2D effects, placing various images inside its screen, while the space scenes adapted shots which had been used earlier in the series. "The green cloudy space was from 'DNA Mad Scientist' and we added asteroids for 'Nerve' and 'The Hidden Memory'," Butterworth adds. "Some of my favourite shots were done at that point, actually."

The biggest new effect, however, was Moya's baby, Talyn. Having waited almost the entire season for the birth, Ricky Eyres knew that all eyes in the audience would be on the offspring. Few could have suspected that Talyn's design would be so radically different from that of his mother. "The design for Talyn came about fairly rapidly," Eyres explains. "I had a wealth of *Farscape* reference — a bible — to draw from. One idea was for the exterior of the ship to be chrome, so that it had an inbuilt cloaking device. Then, when he fired up — in the same way that Moya fires up and the veining appears — there were going to be red lines, so that in space, he'd almost be

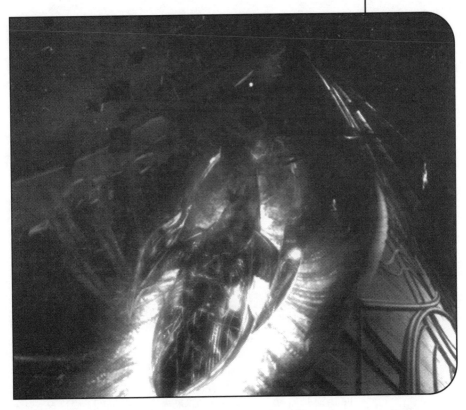

just a reflection, until he fired up and you saw the veining. There were some really cool ideas coming out! Ultimately, what we tried to do with Talyn was imagine that he was either going to be something that looked Peacekeeper-like in Moya's colours, or something that looked Moya-like in Peacekeeper colours. Either way, it was going to be the fusion of the two disciplines — the Peacekeeper style and Moya's style — both of which are very strong. That was why it was such an interesting design. I think what came out of it was pretty stunning," says Eyres proudly.

The addition of weapons to the basic Leviathan design gave room for further creativity. "The original gun turret system, which never really came out, was that Talyn had two turrets, top and bottom, which he's still got, but which had six or seven guns on them, each of which spun independently," says Eyres. "That meant he could fire the weapons in three dimensions, by rolling. Going into attack, he could hit multiple targets coming from different directions. We'll probably see that happening at a later date," Eyres adds. "Plus, he's going to grow, which should be an interesting concept — the set was designed to give him space to grow." ∎

Opposite page:
Scorpius begins to suspect Crais.

Above: *Moya gives birth to Talyn.*

BONE TO BE WILD

Written by: David Kemper & Rockne S. O'Bannon	Guest cast: Lani Tupu (Captain Bialar Crais), Wayne Pygram (Scorpius), Francesca Buller (M'Lee), Marton
Directed by: Andrew Prowse	Csokas (Br'Nee), David Franklin (Lt Braca)

H iding from Captain Crais's Command Carrier in the midst of an asteroid field, and with most of Moya's systems shut down to avoid giving off energy signatures, Pilot picks up a distress call from a nearby asteroid. Crichton, D'Argo and Zhaan take a transport pod to the source of the signal, arriving on a botanical asteroid replete with flora but apparently devoid of animal life. While exploring, however, they encounter a female creature named M'Lee. Though they save her from an attack by a monstrous beast, D'Argo is wounded by it. M'Lee explains how the beast massacred her people, potential colonists of the botanical asteroid. Meanwhile, Pilot reveals to Aeryn that Moya is having problems communicating with her newborn offspring, and asks for her help. Aeryn agrees, and discovers that the interior of the baby matches its exterior — a synthesis of Peacekeeper technology and Leviathan biomechanics. On the asteroid, Crichton learns from Zhaan that Delvians are plant-based life forms, but as he's digesting this revelation, she disappears into the wilderness to look for the plants to cure the wounded D'Argo. Crichton fears that Zhaan has been attacked by the beast, and sets off with M'Lee to its killing ground. But then M'Lee reveals that she is hungry...

Crichton to Zhaan

"You're a plant?"

"Always have been, John. Why, does it bother you?"

"No, it doesn't bother me. I just never suspected... you're a vegetable?"

'Bone to be Wild' contains one of the most startling revelations in *Farscape*'s first season — that Zhaan is a plant. Although no one was more surprised than John Crichton, there were clues during the year. "There would be occasional lines, such as in 'Through the Looking Glass'," Ben Browder points out, "where she was talking about the fibres in her arms,

ENCOUNTERS: M'LEE

Member of a calciferous species which survives by devouring the bones of creatures they have killed. When hungry, the species grow spiky appendages from their bodies, their teeth sharpen into tiny razor-sharp points, and the pale blue translucent nodules around their faces glow bright red. Possessing incredible physical strength, they are only vulnerable after a meal. Their urges can be controlled by drawing upon their calcium reserves.

but most people would not 'twig' to it. When she is revealed as a plant, everybody goes 'Wow,' but the writers had always known that Zhaan was flora, not fauna."

Make-up supervisor Lesley Vanderwalt confirms that the original designs for Zhaan weren't all blue. "Conceptual artist Kevin Harper suggested that her skin colour would change according to her emotions," she explains, "or like a plant that would change colour in different lights. But with the time we had to shoot, that was impossible to do, because it would have held everyone up about two or three hours while we removed Virginia's make-up and painted on different colours."

The episode ended up as Andrew Prowse's favourite of the four he directed in the first year. Ben Browder's wife, actress Francesca Buller, made a great impression in her guest appearance as the calciferous M'Lee. "I just loved working with Fran. Some of the things she did were fabulous," Prowse recalls. "She wanted to do it, because she could see that Ben was having tons of fun on the show," adds Dave Elsey, who designed her remarkable

Above: The calciferous M'Lee.

Next page: Can Crichton and Zhaan trust the botanist Br'Nee?

prosthetic appliances. "But she was very worried, as she didn't want to get cast just because she was Ben's wife — she wanted to audition, and everyone was nervous: 'What do we say to Ben if she's no good?'" Luckily, the problem did not arise. "She was so good in her audition that there was absolutely no doubt," says Elsey. "Nobody else could play M'Lee — she was perfect for it."

"Four episodes, beginning with 'Nerve', were filmed as a block, and we actually scored them as an ongoing piece of music," remembers Chris Neal. "There was a slight step out of the loop when they went down to the botanist's asteroid, and we had to create a different mood for that. We went for a little bit more ambient music, although there was a lot of drama in there with the M'Lee character. The episode was also topped and tailed with Scorpius, so we used our 'Scorpius theme', which had started in 'Nerve', and really ran right through to the end of the season, building in a fairly linear way. So by the time we get to the explosion of the Gammak base at the end of 'Family Ties', it's all guns blazing!" ■

| Written by: Rockne S. O'Bannon & David Kemper Directed by: Tony Tilse | Guest cast: Lani Tupu (Captain Bialar Crais), Wayne Pygram (Scorpius), David Franklin (Lt Braca) |

ith Moya and her offspring still hiding in the asteroid field, but almost certain to be discovered by Crais and Scorpius, Rygel decides to defect to the Peacekeeper Command Carrier and make a deal with Captain Crais — Rygel offers to trade the lives of his companions and the two Leviathans for his own freedom. Crais is in favour of the deal, believing that his brother's death will soon be avenged, but Scorpius, wants to use the traitorous Dominar to reach his true goal: to gain the knowledge of wormhole theory he believes is locked inside Crichton's head. Discovering Rygel's treachery, the crew discuss tactics and Crichton suggests a plan: if Rygel got through Peacekeeper security simply by offering to surrender, might it be possible to pilot a transport pod laden with kronite-injection explosives right into the heart of Crais's ship? D'Argo reluctantly agrees to go along with the plan, and Zhaan begins to formulate a dangerous contact explosive. Going back on his word, Scorpius imprisons Rygel. But Crais, knowing he is losing control of his ship to Scorpius, makes Rygel a surprising offer — he will accompany the Hynerian back to Moya, and seek asylum. Back on the Leviathan, the crew are unsure if they can trust Crais, but to prove his allegiance, he suggests a new plan: rather than the Command Carrier, the explosive-packed transport pod should be aimed at the Gammak base, which is located on an oil-covered moon...

Rygel

"You want the Leviathan, the Leviathan's gunship offspring, the other escaped prisoners, the defector Aeryn Sun, and especially, you want the one called Crichton. Well, I want my freedom. Interested?"

The explosive first season finale grew from a dramatic image in David Kemper's mind. "I wanted to do an episode at the end of the season with Crichton and D'Argo floating in space while a planet is burning behind them. I had to fight for it," he says, "but we ended up doing it! When the Gammak base came up, I said, 'Let's make this an oil covered moon, so the oil is on the surface, and there's just little pockets of land. They've set up a base on the land and they have special air filters because the oil was noxious.'

"Everybody was asking, 'Why does this have to be an oil moon?' But I said, 'Just make it an oil moon,' and I had the CGI people design it that way. I knew that I was going to set the oil on fire at the end of the season! I knew I was going to have to have a transport pod that was a bomb, with

Crichton and D'Argo jumping out, and the pod going down to the planet to ignite it."

Yet despite the slam-bang fireworks of the Gammak base's destruction, Crais's triple betrayal and Scorpius's emergence as the worst villain, 'Family Ties' also provides many quiet moments of emotional significance, making it another favourite among several cast members.

"I loved those final moments," says Anthony Simcoe who, as D'Argo, has perhaps the most poignant scene. "I always find it quite emotional watching that end sequence, not simply because of the emotion of the story, but also because the last shot of season one that we actually filmed was the slow motion shot of D'Argo's hand. They brought down the whole crew — the Creature Shop, construction, and all of admin and production — so there were hundreds of people standing around watching us do this last simple shot. There was big applause and champagne, and it was a touching moment."

"I remember literally crying my heart out on the last day," adds Virginia Hey, recalling her final scenes of the first season. "I get very involved when I'm playing a scene. I call on real emotions. So I thought, 'Well, how would I feel if that was happening in real life? Oh God, I'd feel

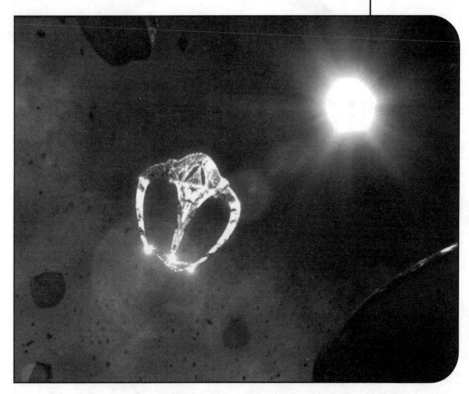

miserable!' So I got myself into a miserable state, and it was very, very moving."

Claudia Black points out an important scene for her character, in which "D'Argo says, 'I always thought I'd live much longer,' and Aeryn replies, 'I never thought I'd live this long.' It was one of the few times that Aeryn cried," Black remembers. "I thought it was a rare moment expressed between them, and an acknowledgement of all they have achieved together." Though she was disappointed that this scene had been trimmed from some broadcast versions of the episode, due to time constraints, Black is happy to know that it is included on the uncut video and DVD release.

Ben Browder recalls that the final line of Crichton's tape-recorded message to his father in 'Family Ties' was originally written, but not used, for the end of the première episode. Now, coming at the end of the season, it had a new resonance. "That last address to Dad is the final evolution of season one," Browder notes. "I reinserted that line Rockne had written — 'This is John Crichton, somewhere in the universe' — and got to hear it in an entirely different way." ■

Opposite page: Crichton and D'Argo are stranded in space...

Above: ... while Moya StarBursts to safety.

THE CHARACTERS

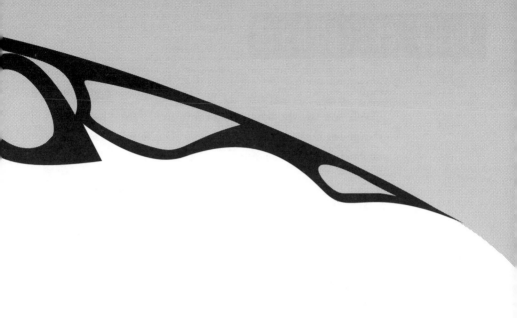

"I have people who rely on me, people who I care about, people who mystify me, and people who've become allies. Friends. And people who teach me patience, and people who teach me other things."

– John Crichton

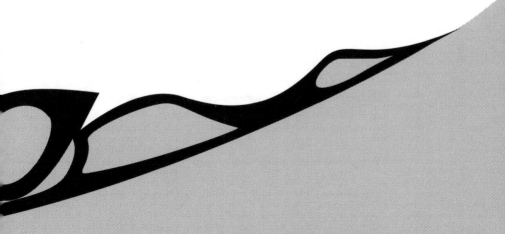

"Well, you said the time would come and I think it has... You did good, Dad. You taught me well. This is John Crichton, somewhere in the universe."

ohn Robert Crichton, Jr. was born in North Carolina, where he would occasionally go fishing with his father, Jack, an astronaut who walked on the moon and was friends with Soviet cosmonaut Yuri Gagarin. Though young Crichton earned a doctorate in Theoretical Sciences, and worked as an astronaut and scientist, he always felt he was somewhat in the shadow of his famous father.

Crichton and his childhood friend DK had a theory: that a manned spacecraft could overcome atmospheric friction and exponentially increase its speed, using only a planet's natural gravitational pull. But during a test flight to prove the theory, Crichton's experimental module, *Farscape 1*, was pulled into a wormhole, transporting him to the other side of the universe. Since then, he has been lost in space, without any known frame of reference, and forced to call upon strengths he never knew he had.

"John Crichton is my favourite character because he stands in for all of us," says series creator Rockne S. O'Bannon. "In *Star Wars*, they meet all sorts of difficulties, but Luke Skywalker knows how to fly, he understands light speed; in *Star Trek*, they may encounter some new alien menace like the Borg, but they know how the transporter works. John Crichton has no idea how anything works! But the one thing he brings to the party is a willingness to stick the knife between his teeth and just dive in, while the others who know the world better may not be willing to do so, because they know the dangers."

The actor chosen to play Crichton, North Carolina-born Ben Browder, was previously best known for playing Neve Campbell's older boyfriend in season three of *Party of Five*. "He had that charm and presence," executive producer David Kemper recalls, "a handsomeness that we knew women would go for, and a sensitivity that they *certainly* go for. He had a heroism, and also a vulnerability that I think men also like, that kind of 'I'm not per-fect' attitude. He was the magic find, because he holds the show together."

Browder saw a noticeable development in John Crichton as the first year progressed. "I break the first season down into three sections," he says. "In the first part you've got 'John the Incompetent', who's really flying by the seat of his pants; he's completely lost. He's just in so far over his head that it's a struggle for him to figure out how to wash his hands and feed himself. Then, in the middle of the season, there's a transition where he becomes more competent and stoic, and that reaches its peak about the time that he goes into the Gammak base in 'Nerve'. He's starting to act like an action

hero, because it's the only way he can intellectually and emotionally deal with the barrage of new things that are thrust upon him. Then he gets thrown in the Aurora Chair, and the effects of that are something that is played out at the end of the season, so at the beginning of the second year, he's a little more volatile.

"In 'A Human Reaction', John Crichton kicks a guy in the head," Browder points out. "It's one of those turning points; something he would never have done in the very beginning. Back then, he was always trying to find an intellectual solution to problems. And by the time you hit 'A Bug's Life', he wilfully kills someone. He's under the influence of the virus, and he's kind of dealing with that, but at the same time, he knows he's going to kill Larraq. And the way he does it — lighting the trail of cesium fuel — means he knows that he's going to kill him, and there's an element that derives satisfaction in taking action in this world in this manner. He's a radically changed man, and the effects of the Chair grab him up and confuse him a little more."

One of Crichton's ways of dealing with events is to make frequent references to Earth's pop culture which only he understands, from Yoda to minty-flavoured dental products, and even *Monty Python*'s deadly "comfy chair." "Ben's shouldered a lot of this responsibility himself," O'Bannon acknowledges. "Some of Crichton's best pop culture ad libs come from him improvising during a take, where he'll say, 'Let me just try, let me just throw this out there.'"

Although Crichton starts out as a complete outsider, Browder feels that his character ultimately becomes the fulcrum for the group. "In the beginning, he's the one who's pleading to hold them together," he explains. "It's a family of his making in some respects; he forces them to look out for one another — 'We're not going to leave people behind. We're not going to dump Rygel. We're going to work together.' And by the end of the season, he has this family forged. In this strange universe where he doesn't understand anything, he's made a family for himself. At the end of 'Family Ties', he says to Zhaan, 'It's a Jerry Springer kind of family, but for what it's worth, you are family.' It's his clan, and it's his safety net against a dangerous universe."

The fact that the rest of the crew comes back for Crichton in 'Jeremiah Crichton' is a key moment in the forging of that family bond. "At that point, he was fed up with being kicked around and treated like a naïve idiot," Browder recalls. "No matter how many times he pulled them back from the brink, they continued to treat him like an idiot. So he goes out for a 'drive' and gets stranded by mistake — but then they come back for him!" Browder thinks that the infinitely more dangerous rescue mission undertaken by Aeryn and D'Argo in 'The Hidden Memory' was even more of a surprise to Crichton. "I don't think he expected even one of them to come back to get him that time," he says. "But I think his attachment and loyalty to them started long before that point. The fact of it being reciprocated is a good thing."

Browder regards Crichton's relationship with Aeryn as "relatively important to the fibre of *Farscape*. But it's not dealt with on a weekly basis, and we like it that way. You will go through three or four episodes where it's not even talked about or addressed; we are just behaving normally. In 'A Human Reaction' they sleep together," he adds, "and there's no mention of it later. They're growing more like each other, in the way couples grow like each other. They're influencing one another. He's becoming more 'take action' than he was, and she's become more thoughtful and sensitive to the people around her. The times when you do focus on them, we take one step, two steps forwards, and one step back," he laughs. "But it's not *Moonlighting*, and it's not Mulder and Scully. It's its own thing." ■

"I was born a Peacekeeper soldier. I've always been one among many... I've never been on my own."

Officer Aeryn Sun — Special Commando, Icarion Company, Pleisar Regiment — is a Sebacean, a race of carbon-based beings. Sebaceans lack the gland necessary to regulate extreme thermal increases and, therefore, must avoid intense heat. If exposed to high temperature for too long, delirium sets in and they ultimately succumb to the 'Living Death', a comatose state from which they never recover. They do not believe in life after death, and are violently opposed to inter-species mating, although they are certainly capable of it. Sebaceans heal quickly, but if they sustain damage to the paraphoral nerve (located near the heart), it cannot regenerate, causing death within a short time unless a tissue graft from a genetically compatible donor is received.

One night, when Aeryn was very young, a scarred, battle-hardened soldier appeared over her bunk. It was her mother, who told her that she was not merely a genetic birthing to fill the ranks, but the rare result of an actual loving relationship: her mother and a male she had cared about had chosen to create a life. That was the only time Aeryn ever saw her mother, and she claims not to know anything about her father except his name, Talyn. A top-notch soldier and combat pilot, Aeryn started flying scrub runners at the age of fourteen cycles. Half a cycle later, she moved on to a KL-80, then an 81, attending Prowler Attack School at sixteen. Piloting one of the Prowlers that was sent from Captain Bialar Crais's Command Carrier to deal with the prison break on board Moya, Aeryn became trapped inside the energy envelope surrounding the escaping Leviathan and was pulled inside the ship when it went into StarBurst. By Peacekeeper standards, her contact with Crichton and the other alien prisoners left her "irreversibly contaminated," making her an outcast from her own people. But her time with Moya's crew has allowed her to finally become a thinking and feeling individual — rather than an anonymous member of a unit.

Originally, Aeryn was to have been a twenty year-old commando who had learned everything by the book. However, in the audition process, casting someone who could carry the role proved very difficult. "Finally, we found Claudia Black," David Kemper recalls. "Rockne and I were watching a tape and Claudia came up and we went, 'That's Aeryn!' She was so strong, and she and Ben Browder were really clicking together."

Australian actress Claudia Black, whose other credits include the science-fiction film *Pitch Black*, had actually been involved in *Farscape* earlier in the audition process, reading lines with actors who were trying out for

other roles on the show. She had been intrigued by the project and was delighted with the screen test opposite Ben Browder: "I remember Anthony Hopkins once saying, 'Learn your lines until it is effortless,' and I felt an enormous sense of effortlessness when I met Ben that day." Claudia was cast, despite the fact that the production schedules on *Pitch Black* and the opening episodes of *Farscape* clashed, meaning much to-ing and fro-ing for the actress: "I remember saying to both production co-ordinators, 'Please make sure I've got vegetarian meals on my flights — my life has been reduced to aeroplane food so please can I have the special meals, otherwise I shan't be eating at all!'"

Claudia believes that Aeryn's emotional journey in *Farscape*'s first season took a while to develop. "Once we got through the first few episodes of season one, my work started to get more grounded," she says, "and in 'PK Tech Girl', the director Tony Tilse really opened up not only the aesthetic of the show, and the spirit and size of the production, but enormous opportunities for me as an actor to play Aeryn. It was where we really started to carve a niche for Aeryn, to show what she was capable of, and I really started to grow from there."

The journey perhaps started a little earlier, with Aeryn's discovery that guns don't solve everything. In 'Thank God It's Friday, Again', she and Pilot begin to form a bond, which is enhanced after Aeryn is injected with some of Pilot's DNA in 'DNA Mad Scientist'. "Pilot was someone with whom Aeryn could start afresh," Claudia reveals, "who she's not met under duress.

Aeryn's very touched by being asked later in the season to name Moya's baby. Pilot has no expectations of her. She's made a lot of mistakes in front of him. He chooses to trust her, and reveals that he doesn't know much himself."

Some of the most telling emotional moments between Aeryn and the other characters have come spontaneously from the actors while shooting a scene. Claudia was particularly pleased that the cameras were filming wide angle for the moment at the end of 'The Flax', when Crichton and Aeryn simultaneously turn and look at each other. "It was pure luck," she recalls. "The turn was completely and utterly unrehearsed." Like Ben Browder, she enjoys the way in which the relationship has grown over the first season. "There is quite a push and pull," she observes. "You need to be able to pull the leads apart, then bring them together, so the audience has an understanding and wants to invest in that relationship, but then create circumstances where they are constantly having conflict about whether it will work."

One of the things that complicate Crichton's and Aeryn's relationship are his feelings about the Peacekeeper tech, Gilina Mays, whom they encounter on the *Zelbinion*, and who later risks everything for Crichton on the Gammak base. "Sebaceans have a caste system which is divided between techs and soldiers," Ben Browder explains, "and the soldiers don't intermingle with the techs. So Aeryn's wondering, 'How can I be interested in you if you're interested in *her*? She's a tech!'" Claudia recalls a discussion with director Tony Tilse about the moment in 'PK Tech Girl' when Aeryn interrupts Crichton and Gilina kissing: "I told Tony I wanted to lift up something really heavy. There's a big difference between saying Aeryn's a hardcore warrior, and showing it. I thought it was a great opportunity to show Aeryn trying to cope with a very awkward situation. In the corridor scene that followed, there was a particular beat where Aeryn concedes that she was attracted to Crichton, and it seemed an odd point for her to open that can of worms, that vulnerability." Unfortunately, the location was rather noisy, meaning that the scene's dialogue had to be dubbed. "I was able to fix the scene in post production," Claudia explains, "and was able to create that moment of vulnerability. When I had to lift the heavy object, I needed to physicalise it in the ADR [additional dialogue recording] booth, so I actually lifted Tony Tilse as my heavy object as I rerecorded that line!" ■

D'Argo

"Fear accompanies the possibility of death. Calm shepherds its certainty."

'Argo is a male of the Luxan species, an aggressive warrior race whose deeply held code of honour — a Luxan cannot lie to an opponent in combat, for example — resembles those of the samurai of feudal Japan. Like many Luxans, D'Argo hides a sensitive and compassionate nature beneath his brash exterior. Luxans also have a highly refined sense of smell and, when injured, cannot begin to heal until their reddish-black blood runs clear.

Several cycles ago, D'Argo secretly married a Sebacean named Lo'Laan, with whom he fathered a son, Jothee. Such marriages being despised in Sebacean culture, Lo'Laan's scandalised brother, a Peacekeeper named Macton Tar, brutally murdered her and framed the devastated D'Argo for the crime. D'Argo managed to get Jothee to safety before he was imprisoned by the Peacekeepers and has been yearning ever since to see his son again. As a boy, D'Argo dreamed of serving aboard a Luxan Assault Piercer, and earning military honours like those of his ancestors: his great-grandfather died in a war against the Teloks after withstanding a siege for more than 100 solar days. D'Argo's weapon is the Qualta Blade, a powerful Luxan design which can be used as a sword or pulse rifle.

Series creator Rockne S. O'Bannon points out that initial reactions to the character can be deceptive. "When people first watch the show there tends to often be a kind of arms-crossed, 'Well, D'Argo's the Klingon and Zhaan's Obi Wan Kenobi,'" he says. "But then, as it goes on, people start to see them as distinct from those icons." It is D'Argo's appearance that first makes an impact on the viewer (discussed in detail in the Creature Shop chapter). Costume designer Terry Ryan explains that there were practical reasons for not weighing down the Luxan warrior with heavy body armour and lots of weaponry. "He's quite big anyway," Ryan observes, "and he's got that head and tentacles already, so if we had given him much more, he would have looked really 'busy'. We went sort of Celtic with him, to start with, and made D'Argo look more like a Viking, adding eclectic touches such as that pseudo-Japanese quilted tunic. Who knows though, we may go back to the Celtic look again."

As the man under the Luxan warrior's skin, Australian actor Anthony Simcoe should know him better than anyone. So how would he describe D'Argo? "I would say he's like a teenager, locked in a warrior's body," Simcoe offers. "He's an adolescent who wants to prove himself to the world in the most inappropriate ways. But then, in his more private moments, you find out that he's actually much softer and more soulful than his position in life makes him appear to be. I'm always really happy when they're willing to push D'Argo

further and further away from the warrior. I like the fact that he's brash, ill-tempered and perhaps irresponsible and naïve at times, and that does make those warrior qualities come out. But he's much more interesting as a character when his interactions with other people are softer, guided more from positive sentiment, and wanting to connect with people, to explore their thoughts, feelings and psychologies."

Simcoe, perhaps best known before *Farscape* for his role in the hit comedy film *The Castle*, admits that he knew little about D'Argo when he first auditioned. "I didn't know what he was going to look like," he says. "I didn't even know I was going to be in prosthetics!" In fact, one of the few things the actor *was* told was changed by the time production commenced. "D'Argo's whole backstory was completely different when they were first putting together *Space Chase*," Simcoe reveals. "Originally he was going to be portrayed as a general, and much older, and have a backstory in which he was framed by another general. But they didn't feel that it made him vulnerable enough, so they said, 'It's much more interesting if we made him a lot younger,' and fleshed out this other backstory, about his wife and Jothee."

A more fundamental change came during production of the first episode. "I auditioned for D'Argo with a quite neutral English accent," Simcoe recalls, "but when I saw the make-up, I thought, 'Well, this really isn't going to wash!' And then, when we were rehearsing without the make-up, I knew the producers were panicking. They were thinking,

'Why have we cast Anthony Simcoe? Something doesn't equate here!' I said, 'Look, it's the voice,'" Simcoe says, switching from his own soft Australian tones to D'Argo's distinctive rumble, "'D'ARGO *HAS TO SPEAK LIKE THIS!'* And because it came out of my own face at that rehearsal, rather than D'Argo's, they were like, 'No way, there's no way you can do it like that!'" However, once the actor was in his full prosthetic make-up and costume, the producers were convinced. "It was a real last-minute decision," Simcoe says, "but it created that synergy between the mask and the voice."

D'Argo underwent yet another slight transformation during the production of 'Throne for a Loss'. In the first three episodes to be shot, 'Premiere', 'I, E.T.' and 'Exodus from Genesis', "D'Argo's got green contact lenses in," Simcoe reveals. But a mishap forced the actor to stop using the lenses: "One day we were taking the make-up off and I mistakenly opened my eyes, and all this alcohol went into them, and actually burned the corneas! It was completely my fault — we have wonderful, very responsible make-up people — but I was rushed to hospital, and blindfolded for two days, with friends leading me round the house!"

Since losing the lenses, Simcoe has found that, with most of his face and body hidden behind prosthetics, he prefers to use his own eyes. "I think it works much better for the character," he says, "because you read so much more of his vulnerability through the dilation of the pupils. Virginia wears contacts to play Zhaan, and the fact that you can't read her eyes actually helps with her austere priest-like aura. But I like the opposite for D'Argo, and not having the contacts allows me to breathe a little more vulnerability and soulfulness into the character." Simcoe feels that it is this duality which makes D'Argo interesting. "You could never get bored on a show like *Farscape*," he states, "but you could certainly get *comfortable*. I like to make sure that I don't feel comfortable inside D'Argo, in the sense that I'm trying to twist myself in every episode into some new direction, just for the sake of finding new boundaries for him as a person."

Of course, with layers of prosthetics to be applied every day, being too comfortable is one problem Simcoe will probably never have playing D'Argo. "But the great thing about wearing that type of prosthetic is that you get a lot for free," he observes. "I just have to trust the make-up and walk into frame!" ■

Zhaan

"On my home world, even among my kind, I was something of an anarchist. Actually, I was the leading anarchist."

Delvians — a plant species — are highly evolved beings, and have numerous abilities linked to their spiritual side. Many, like Zhaan, train as priests — or Pa'u — in the Delvian Seek. Pa'u are able to share the pain of others by laying on hands, meld mind and soul with another through a spiritual procedure known as 'Unity', and perform manual tasks at remarkable speeds. Delvians are unusually sensitive to ionic radiation, which provokes a form of sexual euphoria referred to as 'photogasms'. However, they also can succumb to their darker impulses, causing their eyes to turn red and their minds to snap.

Zhaan reached the Ninth Plateau in the Delvian Seek while imprisoned for killing her lover, Bitaal, a spiritual counsellor who betrayed the Delvians by conspiring with the Peacekeepers in a *coup d'état*. "No one really knows exactly what the Delvian priesthood involves," says Virginia Hey, the actress beneath the character's head-to-toe make-up. "Zhaan is very knowledgeable in many areas, but we don't know at this stage whether all of those areas — medicine, science and so forth — are part of the priesthood, or whether they're just individual things that she's studied along the way."

Since escaping imprisonment aboard Moya, Zhaan has demonstrated two sides to her character, indicating the duality of her complex personality: although she is a compassionate and spiritual person, she also has a dark side and, if necessary, will go to extreme lengths to serve her own ends — even if it means cutting off one of Pilot's arms, as happens in 'DNA Mad Scientist'. "She's incredibly logical," Hey comments, defending the move, "and it was a logical thing to do. In order to save lives, something has to be sacrificed. Besides, Pilot's arm will grow back, like a lizard's tail." Eventually.

Hey, best known outside of her native Australia as 'Warrior Woman' in the second *Mad Max* film, recalls what she was told about Zhaan when she first auditioned for the role — and, more importantly, what she *wasn't* told. "On the breakdown the casting agents sent for Zhaan, I think it said simply, 'fit; strong; statuesque'. They didn't mention 'blue' or 'bald' or anything like that! But it was such a massive show, and people were being brought in from all over the world to put it together, so it's not surprising that details — even really important details! — got missed." Hey says that she learned the most about the character from reading the audition pieces, "challenging some alien, and, in the middle of a battle, trying to make a very quick decision about which war tactic to follow. But I wasn't given any backstory as such, because there was no detailed *Farscape* 'bible' at that stage.

"I was curious to find out more," she continues, "and the possibility of playing some kind of a spiritual character appealed to me. I follow Eastern philosophies in my private life, and I also have been studying natural healing pretty much all my life, but in a concentrated form in the last ten years. So when I found out through the audition pieces that she was also a doctor, and a scientist, I thought, 'Oh my God, all these things I love!'" The character developed through the audition process, during which, she says, "you're basically a piece of plasticene, and you're being moulded by the various casting directors. Each time you audition, the casting agent would suggest a different way of presenting it."

The next important stage was to devise Zhann's make-up and hair — or lack of it. "I'm not naturally bald," Hey laughs. "I'm bald for the sake of art, at the moment. Actors are always altering themselves. This is a rather radical alteration, I admit, but they didn't ask me to alter my body. If someone asked me to put on thirty or forty pounds for a role, like Robert De Niro did for his part in *Raging Bull* or Russell Crowe did in *The Insider*, I would have to say, 'No way,' because that would really screw up your whole digestive system and really take a toll on your endocrine system — they'd be completely tospy-turvy. In comparison with that, it's more like a man shaving off his beard, and it doesn't affect me in any way."

Besides, she says, "it's one of the main reasons, if not *the* reason, why

Zhaan looks so extraordinary, because hardly anyone else has done that. There's Sinead O'Connor, but she's still got her eyebrows! Zhaan's a very popular character, but visually she's very unusual, and it's because she doesn't look like anything else. She doesn't look human, and yet it's quite an elegant and beautiful make-up. I'm actually quite proud of myself for taking the artistic risk," she says, adding that she does not believe she would have shaved her head for a lesser role, or a lesser production. "If *Farscape* wasn't successful, I could have made a huge fool of myself!"

As for the prosthetic make-up, "It's very easy to wear because the only prosthetics are little tiny pieces attached to my ear lobes and behind my jaw," Hey reveals. The entire process — including her all-over body paint — takes around three hours to apply. "It's three hours of sitting absolutely still. You can't move your head; you have to keep your head upright and look ahead. But it's really my only social time, because the rest of the day is heads down and bums up — we're really flying. It's like we're making a feature film every week — and an expensive one, at that — and you're just trying to concentrate on what you're doing, and trying to keep the dialogue in your head." While the make-up is not exactly uncomfortable to wear, Hey admits that it does present her with certain difficulties. "I haven't blown my nose in two years," she laughs, "not whilst in make-up anyway! Can you imagine the almighty mess that would create for the make-up girls?"

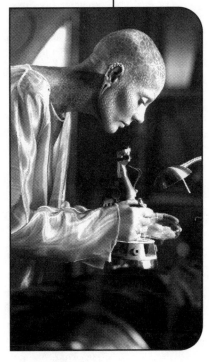

Zhaan's clothing adds the finishing touches to her character. Costume designer Terry Ryan explains the thinking that went into the look. "The big thing was getting her make-up right," he says, "to get the right blue, because if you then put a costume that's too blue on her, she just bounces out of the screen, but if you put on something too grey, then her head tends to stand out, and not her body. So it was waiting to get that right blue. She's sort of the big hippie of the piece, and because Hey is an ex-model, and statuesque, we wanted her to be sensual and kind of drapey. Whereas everybody else among the crew can come across as aggressive, she's this fluid presence who keeps everything together in a sort of cosmic way." But, as Ryan points out, the costume had to be durable, and ready for action: "There were also practical issues. She has to be able to fight, and run a ship — you can't just have her wafting around looking too gorgeous!" ∎

"What you need on this jaunt is a talented burglar and distraction-causer!"

"Chiana was named after my wife Liana," reveals Rockne S. O'Bannon, "but we changed the beginning to a 'Ch' to give it a slightly harder sound." Chiana is a street-smart, mercurial, flirtatious, troublesome, teenage Nebari. She was first brought aboard Moya as a prisoner, having been arrested for behaving and speaking in ways that are not acceptable on her planet. Since escaping her Nebari captors and deciding to stay aboard Moya — at least, for as long as it suits her — Chiana has lied, cheated, vamped and scammed her way out of many situations. Fortunately for her, that's what she does best.

Chiana's colouring and feline movements give her appearance the suggestion of a black and white cat. "She's almost totally black and white," agrees costume designer Terry Ryan, who notes that the lighting can often make it seem otherwise. "She's not completely monochromatic, because in order to get those shades of grey to blend, you've got to have them so that some are a bit blue, and some are a bit brown. It just takes that really sharp edge off it. She looks a bit more real. Without softening those colours a bit, because she's so tiny, Chiana ran the risk of looking like one of those Japanese cartoon characters."

Chiana is played by Australian actress Gigi Edgley, whose awareness of The Jim Henson Company came many years before she won her role on *Farscape*. "Ever since I was a young girl, I'd grown up watching *The Dark Crystal*, *Labyrinth*, *The Storyteller* and stuff like that," she says, "and I'd always believed in the underworld and the imagination, so being a part of that, and working with Rygel and Pilot, is absolutely unbelievable. Obviously someone's looking after me up top. Thank you, universe!"

Edgley "fell into the role" of Chiana during her third and final year studying drama at university. "A casting agent came to talk to us, and she said, 'You, you and you, you're coming for a casting.'" Edgley read for a part in a local mini-series, *Day of the Roses*, which led to her getting an agent, which ultimately led to a regular role on *Farscape* — that is, after a few five-hour make-up tests. "I had no idea when I did the initial auditions that there was such intense make-up work with her," she admits, "no idea of the extent and the time and energy that was going to be put into her. I went into the first make-up test, which was about five-and-a-half hours long, and as layer upon layer went on, I was just laughing, crying and everything, and they were saying, 'Sit in the seat, you've got a few more hours yet!' And then, suddenly, there was Chiana in the mirror, and

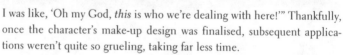

I was like, 'Oh my God, *this* is who we're dealing with here!'" Thankfully, once the character's make-up design was finalised, subsequent applications weren't quite so grueling, taking far less time.

Edgley says that during the filming of her first episode, 'Durka Returns', she was unaware that Chiana had initially begun as a 'one-episode wonder'. "I had no idea. Right at the end of that episode, Durka fires off a shot, and the bullet kind of slices her arm, just enough to draw blood. When we were at the wrap party for the first season, David Kemper said, 'You know that bullet... That was meant to kill you!' And I said, 'Thanks! It's as easy as that, is it?' One line in the script — either, 'bullet hits, Chiana dies,' or 'bullet scrapes her arm, Chiana becomes a regular!'

"I think Chiana is very mercurial," Edgley continues. "She's totally out for herself. She lives, she fights, she eats, and she cries for herself, to live, for survival — and I think she has as much fun as she can along the way. Quite often, there is definitely a *naïveté* about her, and she doesn't understand why a kiss isn't just a kiss, for example, when that is her way of thanking people! It's just another one of her characteristics. The writers will come to me with these ideas, some of which will be pretty nasty, and I'll say, 'Oh, man! People will absolutely *hate* Chiana, what are you doing to her?' And they'll reply, 'That's what aliens do!'"

Edgley feels that the character has definitely evolved since the earlier auditions. "Originally, she was much more naturalistic," Edgley explains, "because they just wanted to see if I could act! She definitely had some cheek in her, and a bit of raunch, but she didn't have any of the head movements, or the breath work, nothing like that. But I saw how the 'guesties' came in and got these fantastic make-ups, but still did very naturalistic acting, and I thought, 'That's interesting!' If you've got all this time and energy spent on you, all you have to do is a look to the right with a bit of a breath," she adds, describing techniques she has used in her performance, "and you've got an alien there."

In the early days, Edgley confesses that she did not even know who was a puppet and who was an actor. "I didn't have a clue," she laughs. "I'd watched a few episodes of *Far-scape*, but the first time I watched it, I could not tell who was inside the bodies and what was a puppet. It was so well polished to me." Although Edgley initially had reservations about acting opposite a puppet — "I was really scared, because they don't have the connection in the eyes, and that's one thing I usually try to do to make it real, make eye contact" — these fears were allayed after her first scene with Rygel: "The first day I worked with him, I just came off going, 'Oh my God, I think he did a better job!'"

So where does Chiana go from here? "I think now that she knows the crewmembers a bit more, and she's relaxed a lot, she's going to be a lot more conversational in the future," Edgley says. "I think the alien still pops out in her, when she's meeting or sussing out a new person, or she's in a stand-off or whatever. I'm trying to find that balance again, to bring the alien in enough to make her something from another world, but still be watchable."

Terry Ryan understands the paradox. "Because she's such a con artist, she needs to have that 'street cred'," he says, "but she also needed to be softened up somehow, so that she can take you in. She can really have that girlie sweetness to her, but she'll be picking your pockets at the same time!" ∎

"I am Rygel XVI. Dominar to over six hundred billion people. I don't need to talk to you."

Fluffy. Spanky. Sparky. Buckwheat the Sixteenth — these are just some of the names Crichton has bestowed on Moya's resident pain in the eema, Dominar Rygel XVI. Rygel once lived a life of luxury on Hyneria, an aquatic planet where he was waited on hand and foot by thousands of servants, most of them female. Rygel claims his mother found him the most handsome of her children, and banished his older brothers.

Ever since being deposed from his throne by his cousin Bishan hundreds of cycles ago, Rygel has been a prisoner of the Peacekeepers. He was originally taken on board the *Zelbinion*, where he was tortured by Captain Selto Durka, an experience that left him with nightmares, although he maintains that Durka never broke him.

During more than 130 cycles of incarceration, Rygel may no longer have loyal subjects and servants kowtowing to him, but he does discover a heretofore unknown talent: a gift for negotiation and bribery. Though he is often successful in securing much needed supplies for Moya and the crew (and, of course, secretly hoarding some for himself), at other times his wheeling and dealing lands them all in trouble. When he can't trade for what he wants, Rygel has no qualms about stealing, or as he prefers to call it, "procuring." This dubious "talent" gives him something in common with Chiana — who's not adverse to a bit of "snurching" herself. With a gift for annoying the others — partly by farting helium when upset, but mostly because of his egomaniacal behaviour and superior attitude — Rygel is usually exasperating, but also oddly endearing...

A creation of Jim Henson's Creature Shop, Rygel was brought to life in the first season through the skills of British puppeteer John Eccleston — best known in the UK for his irrepressible puppet characters, Mr Sage and Mr Onion, on the BBC's *Live and Kicking* show. "They wanted him to be small, but with big ideas and a big attitude," Eccleston recalls. "The whole idea of him being a Dominar, or a king, on his own planet was the key thing: grand ideas, small character." Eccleston spent a year in Australia contorting his tall frame into the oddest positions to achieve the necessary shots for Rygel. "I would talk through the scene with the directors," he explains. "I'd sit where Rygel was going to sit, performing with the other actors, and I would carry a little rubber puppet so that they got the eye-level right. The big problem was the limitations of what Rygel can do physically in any one sequence. Because he's so small, there's actually nowhere for me to hide. I'm six foot one and fourteen stone, and the puppet's only two feet high!"

So how did Eccleston operate Rygel? "One hand was inside the head operating the mouth, and my other hand was down on the lip control cable. Then there were other guys operating his hands. The puppet's cable system had always been designed to work with the puppeteer 'underneath' the set, but then the producers decided that they weren't going to build the sets raised off the floor. So we had to do everything at floor level, and I was usually under the table, lying on my side. We built lots of little rigs to accommodate me, and we ended up having to use two other guys, to do one hand each. Suddenly, it's gone from being one person to three people, sometimes even four people, and it's like an iceberg: there's only one tenth of you above the table, and the rest of you just splays out across the floor! You couldn't shoot from a high angle because you would see me, so it had to be low, and it couldn't be too wide because you'd see the cable."

Consequently, Rygel doesn't move around very much. For the occasional scene where it was really necessary, alternative methods were used. Paul Butterworth and the Garner McLellan visual-effects team created a 3D computer model of Rygel (see CGI section), which débuted in

'Exodus from Genesis' and also was used to perform the more complicated movements in 'Jeremiah Crichton'.

Eccleston grew rather fond of Rygel — up to a point. "He's a great character to watch," the puppeteer laughs, "you love him and the situations he gets into, but you wouldn't want him as a friend!" To aid the other actors, Eccleston also provided Rygel's voice when filming on set, but knew that this guide performance would be overdubbed. Classically trained New Zealand actor and Oscar nominee, Jonathan Hardy, auditioned for the vocal role and was awarded the part of the "unkingly king."

Voicing the LRC (short for Little Rubber Chappie, Rygel's nickname) can be a complicated business. Hardy spends about two days per episode in a studio with post production sound engineer Angus Robertson. Hardy has tremendous admiration for the skills of the puppeteers, who manipulate Rygel's throat 'muscles' to produce the correct contractions for the necessary vowel sounds. "That's the great thing about voicing the puppet," Hardy notes. "It's so dynamic. It justifies a lot of vocal work that you can't put into a normal humanoid character."

"Sometimes it's very straightforward," Hardy says of the dubbing sessions, "but there are other times that are difficult. The puppeteers may lay down a voice track and I then have to treat the other actors as if I was on stage, and listen to them very carefully so I get the interplay with their voices exact. Obviously, the way they inflect something affects Rygel's reply. What I have to do is hard enough, but Angus has to take what I've done and get it to match up with Rygel's lips *and* stay with the guide track. If the puppeteer gets carried away with the dramatics of it, we have to go with him. I'm an actor, not a puppeteer. We have to take what's there, and I either enhance that or change that, depending on the relationship with the other actors."

Seeing himself as the guardian of his character, Hardy makes excuses for Rygel's behaviour by saying he's "misunderstood! His upbringing means he has things that look like faults in an alien environment," Hardy says with a laugh. "I, however, think he's perfect." ∎

Above: Puppeteer John Eccleston on location — and in costume — for the episode 'Jeremiah Crichton'.

"We are most fulfilled when serving others. Your presence is gratifying and comforting."

"Y ou know, this ship is amazing!" Crichton's initial reaction to his new home is hardly surprising. Moya and her symbiotic Pilot are far more than just a mode of transport. Moya is a living ship, a member of a bio-mechanoid race known as Leviathans. A huge, oval-shaped being with three tendril sections that meet in a point at the end, Moya is sentient, has emotions, and can feel pain.

Born free, Moya was captured by Leviathan hunters and sold to the Peacekeepers to be used as a prison. Subduing them with a highly potent sleep agent (a process which the weak and the old do not survive), Peacekeepers modify the propulsion and guidance systems of enslaved Leviathans, and fit them with control collars. The collar prevents the Leviathan and Pilot from taking any action against the will of their captors. The Peacekeepers also install a Paddac Beacon hidden deep inside the Leviathan which broadcasts their position unless the Peacekeepers receive a regular signal from the control collar. In lieu of using control collars, the Peacekeepers have experimented with a neural control on Leviathan Pilots but, so far, this has not been successful.

Leviathans contain transport pods for short shuttle trips to planets or other ships. They also are equipped with a docking web, an energy field that can draw smaller ships inside the larger Leviathan. Leviathans are unarmed, but to elude danger, they use a defensive manoeuvre called StarBurst — an ability to enter the seam between space-time dimensions. The ship simply rides out the energy stream until it is randomly pushed back out into normal space.

Like all living beings, Leviathans reproduce. Little is known about the gestation period (even Pilots are not privy to any special knowledge), but the crew of Moya get first-hand experience of it when they realise that their ship is pregnant. Moya's first concern is for her baby, leading her to initially neglect the needs of everyone else on board so she can channel resources to her child.

As the crew are shocked to discover, Moya's baby is a hybrid — half Peacekeeper warship, half Leviathan. Talyn, as the child is later named, is a fusion of Peacekeeper technology and bio-mechanics — yielding a potentially deadly weapon with a mind of his own.

Pilot, like all of his kind, is an independent entity who operates symbiotically with his Leviathan host. Inhabiting a chamber deep within the Leviathan, he is physically joined to Moya. The lower part of his body is

made up of neural tendrils which are threaded through and fused with Moya's systems. Pilot acts as Moya's control centre and navigator, monitoring and maintaining all of her systems, based on constant updates from the DRDs (Diagnostic Repair Drones) which act as his eyes and ears all over the ship. Pilot's bond with Moya means that he can feel much of what she feels, and can communicate her thoughts to the rest of the crew. Although a Leviathan's course is normally guided by the ship's Pilot, manual flight by other crew members is possible.

Because Pilot's species are incapable of interstellar travel on their own, they join with a host Leviathan in order to reach the stars. The price? Living in service to the ship and its crew at all times — an arrangement that Pilot finds perfectly equitable, though his loyalty is to Moya first, and the others second.

New Zealand-born actor Lani Tupu voices Pilot, in a performance that's quite a contrast to his onscreen *Farscape* role as Crais. Tupu's soft tones accompany the many arm-waving motions and spectacularly detailed facial movements of the huge and highly complex animatronic Creature Shop creation, controlled by a team of seven puppeteers under the command of Sean Masterson.

Tupu remembers his intitial discussion with the producers when he auditioned for the role: "The idea they gave me to play with was that Pilot

was like a very harassed accountant." Tupu now sees Pilot as just as much of an explorer as the others aboard Moya. "Pilot is as adventurous as any of the other characters in the series," he says. "He really does want to see as much of the universe as possible, while taking care of Moya and making sure that she is safe. During the first season, you don't really know where he comes from, and you don't quite know who he is. You just know he fulfills his function. I rather think he tends to consider most of the others as being grown-up babies.

"Pilot likes Aeryn a lot," Tupu says, "although initially there was a suspicion that 'once a Peacekeeper, always a Peacekeeper.' But he's been through a lot with Aeryn, and a wonderful relationship has been set up there. He responds really well to Crichton and he has a good relationship with Zhaan, and later on with Chiana, too, though he doesn't really have much contact with her until the birth of Moya's baby."

For the first block of filming, Tupu worked on set with the other actors, but it soon proved simpler for him to record his lines in a separate session. "I really liked that aspect of being on set though," he says, "because my response was different from any one of the puppeteers who were moving Pilot at the time. Unfortunately, it's just not physically possible to do, especially if I'm working as Crais as well." ■

Rockne S. O'Bannon

"Some characters you just know you're going to have to bring back."

Bialar Crais was born in a Sebacean farming community. In his eighth or ninth cycle, he and his younger brother, Tauvo, who had been left in Bialar's care, were shanghaied by Peacekeeper recruiters. Many cycles later, and now a Peacekeeper captain, Bialar was delighted when Tauvo was assigned to his Command Carrier. However, when the Carrier's Prowlers are unleashed in pursuit of Moya, Crichton's ship, *Farscape 1*, appears through a wormhole, into their path. Tauvo is killed instantly when his Prowler collides with Crichton's shuttle, spins out of control and is destroyed.

Crais

"Tauvo is dead, struck down by a weak, pathetic, inferior being. It must be avenged! I swear in Tauvo's name, Crichton, you will die in my hands!"

From the moment Bialar Crais learns of his brother's death, he begins to lose control of his life. Gaining permission from the Peacekeeper Council to enter the Uncharted Territories, Crais's obsession to find Crichton intensifies. His first plan — using a Marauder with crack commandos to locate Moya — fails when the team are ambushed by Crichton, working with the Drak Monarch. When Peacekeeper Admiral Josbek orders him via message chip to return from the Uncharted Territories, Crais refuses. He destroys the chip, and kills his second in command, Lieutenant Teeg, who had witnessed the instruction.

After meeting Crichton face to face in a psychic duel arranged by Maldis, Crais, his obsession fuelled still further, sends out holographic wanted beacons to encourage bounty hunters to capture the fugitives. It is some time before the crew of Moya encounter him again, on the Gammak base. When Gilina's deception leads Scorpius to put Crais in the Aurora Chair, Scorpius learns of Lieutenant Teeg's murder, and uses this information to bend the captain to his will, assuming control of Crais's Command Carrier.

Captain Crais is played by Lani Tupu, a classically trained actor who originally auditioned for the part of D'Argo. And though Anthony Simcoe won the role, executive producer David Kemper was unwilling to let Tupu get away. "I said to Rock, 'We shouldn't lose Lani. Why don't we have him read as Crais?' He had that goatee, and I thought that would be a cool evil look." In fact, the beard was part of the style required for another production that Tupu was filming, and which overlapped with his early *Farscape* appearances. As the season progressed, and Crais became more of a renegade, make-up supervisor Lesley Vanderwalt allowed a wilder

look: "I think the idea was that he got so caught up with looking for Crichton, that he would start to lose his military side. We made him looser, and sweatier, and darker under the eyes, just so it looked like he was losing his mind a bit!"

Tupu sees Crais as "unpredictable" and "having great passion, which becomes a flaw, because he gives up everything to capture Crichton." For Crais, that might include a relationship... with Aeryn. Before filming the scene between the two characters in the première, Tupu and Claudia Black discussed the possibility that Crais might be attracted to Aeryn, and Tupu coloured his performance accordingly. "I said to her, 'I'm playing it from a point of view that I'm attracted to you, but I'm not going to let you know about that,'" Tupu recalls. "We hadn't told anyone, but later on we mentioned it to one of the directors and the writers, and of course they picked it up."

"In an ideal world," Tupu adds, "since Crais hasn't really got a buddy, it would be great for him and Crichton to be friends." However, Ben Browder feels that there is no chance of that for his character. "Crais has a capacity to really push Crichton's buttons," says Browder. "By the time Crais is ready to be reasonable, Crichton doesn't want anything to do with him. He doesn't think that Crais has changed. He's like the guy who bullied you in the schoolyard, and you never really forgive that guy."

Little is known about **Scorpius**, the Scarran-Sebacean half-breed who has unconditional authority on the Peacekeeper's top-secret Gammak base. His physical appearance is calculated to scare, and the aura of power that surrounds him keeps most people in check. Scorpius is a scientist, totally dedicated to his mission — to discover the secrets of wormhole technology. When he discovers Crichton on his base, he uses information from the Aurora Chair to map Crichton's neural pathways, and to his delight he learns that the human actually appears to have the wormhole knowledge he seeks.

Scorpius was one of the original characters envisaged for *Farscape*, though he was initially conceived as a fully animatronic insect-like creature. Australian actor and musician Wayne Pygram, the man beneath Dave Elsey's prosthetics and Terry Ryan's costume for Scorpius, came to *Farscape* through the standard audition process. "Scorpius was pitched as a malevolent Spock," Pygram recalls, referring to the original *Star Trek*'s highly intelligent and logical First Officer. "He wants wormhole technology, and he thinks Crichton has it. Crichton's like the person who was the first to understand the splitting of the atom here on Earth. To Scorpius, wormhole technology is like the splitting of the atom

Scorpius

"I care a great deal about one thing: the knowledge of wormhole technologies the human Crichton holds locked in his memory."

— whoever gets there first is going to be the most powerful person in that part of the universe."

Scorpius doesn't seem to have any redeeming features. "But maybe in his world you can't just look at things through human eyes," Pygram suggests. "He's certainly entertaining; certainly very cheeky! He's a sexy brute! That might be explored in the future — there's talk of him having a partner, and what happens in that area of his life. He's only going to serve himself," he adds, "but if serving himself happens to mean saving someone else's life, or improving other people's lives, so be it. He's the sort of guy who could do that; he's in a powerful position, so maybe he has moments of benevolence. So long as it serves himself."

During the making of the four first-season episodes in which Scorpius appears, the make-up initially took about two and a half hours to apply. "But we've got it down to about an hour and fifteen minutes, which is fantastic," Pygram says gratefully. "Dave Elsey's boys are so sharp, they do not stop finessing the make-up, and it's got very quick and much more comfortable." In those early episodes, however, the prosthetics and headgear were heavy to wear. "It was mainly the black helmet that was originally quite heavy, and very, very tight," Pygram laments. "I'd get headaches after only about three or four hours and my ears would ache. I don't know what it weighed, but my neck would get sore. It was like wearing a motorcycle helmet, and when you're wearing something like that on a long day, you're going to become aware of it eventually. It's an impediment to certain things. When we're finished, it takes half an hour to get all cleaned up — it's a fabulous feeling getting it all off at the end of the day!"

Jack Crichton, played by American actor Kent McCord, has left footsteps so large that his son John doubts he can ever fill them. But Jack Crichton knows he was not always an attentive father. He was often away at critical times in his son's life, although on one birthday, he moved heaven and earth to get home in time to take his son fishing, and has always had enormous pride in John's achievements.

> **Jack Crichton to John Crichton**
>
> "Each man gets the chance to be his own kind of hero. Your time will come and when it does, watch out. Chances are, it'll be the last thing you ever expected."

Kent McCord has known executive producer David Kemper since playing an astronaut on *seaQuest DSV*. When the producers had difficulty casting Jack Crichton, Kemper called, McCord says, "at 2 am and said, 'It's David. You doing anything this week?' And I said, 'Not that I know of.'" Kemper told McCord about the role, asked if McCord was interested, and if he had a valid passport. "Kemper says, 'Can you be on a plane tonight?' So I hop on a plane, film the episode, and fly back — I was only away from home for a total of 105 hours!

"As an actor I could look at Ben Browder as John," McCord considers, "and I could love him like my son. I would want him protected and I would do anything that I could to save him from any danger. I think that's all that had to be expressed in that scene," he says of his role in the première episode. McCord's second *Farscape* appearance, in 'A Human Reaction', required him to play one of the Ancients, the race who test John to see how human-ity will react to an alien presence, in the form of Jack Crichton. "I asked, 'Do we want the audience to know that I'm alien?'" McCord recalls. "Do I do the odd blink of the eye or something that's off-kilter? They said, 'No, we don't want to give away the ending.' So all I had to do was fill that character with 'me' again."

Gilina Mays, the pretty Peacekeeper Maintenance Provost Technician based aboard Bialar Crais's Command Carrier, was left behind on the *Zelbinion* while running a tech sweep of the derelict ship. Gilina immediately recognised the "traitor", Officer Aeryn Sun, and the rest of the "escaped prisoners" when they boarded the *Zelbinion*, but she set aside her prejudices and agreed to help Crichton, with whom she began to share a mutual attraction.

After repairing the *Zelbinion*'s defence shield — and ingeniously extending its coverage area to Moya to fend off the Sheyang attack — Crichton and Gilina reluctantly parted, despite their growing affection for each other. Gilina agreed to remain behind on the *Zelbinion* to await Crais's return, promising not to reveal that she had ever encountered Crichton or Aeryn.

Although Gilina thought she would never see Crichton again, Crais's vendetta against the human causes their paths to cross once more, on the Gammak base. She synthesises the tissue sample necessary for saving Aeryn, and later helps Crichton escape from Scorpius's custody, but Gilina dies heroically after being shot by the evil half-breed. Although there can be little doubt that Gilina had fallen in love with Crichton, she believed that it was Aeryn whom he truly loved, and was willing to sacrifice herself so that they could be together.

Gilina Mays was memorably portrayed by Alyssa-Jane Cook, well-known in her native Australia as both an actress (she was a regular on *E Street*) and television presenter.

Gilina

"I have been sworn never to compromise Peacekeeper technology with the enemy. I will do it for you. For all of you."

Battle-scarred and half-blind, **Selto Durka** was once the captain of the Peacekeeper Command Carrier *Zelbinion*. His exploits, including the liberation of Mintaka 3 and the quelling of the Cenobian rebellion, were legendary. Durka was believed lost along with his ship when the *Zelbinion* was virtually destroyed during an engagement

Durka

"Hello, Rygel. You undid the Nebari mental cleansing – isn't that the most superb irony?"

with a Nebari host vessel. The discovery of the *Zelbinion* resurrects Rygel's worst memories of his former torturer, and the Hynerian refuses to believe that Durka is dead until he sees the Peacekeeper's body with his own eyes. Rygel finally finds what appears to be Durka's corpse, along with evidence that he had shot himself as his ship was outgunned by the Nebari. Rygel demonstrates his contempt for the brutal captain by spitting on his desiccated corpse.

It is not long, however, before Rygel has to face his demons once more, as he comes face to face with Durka, very much alive, and now sporting a black eye-patch and long white hair. Far from perishing by his own hand aboard the *Zelbinion*, the Captain had faked his death and deserted his stricken ship in an escape pod. Following his escape, he was captured by the Nebari, who placed him in cryonic suspension for 100 cycles, and used their notorious corrective

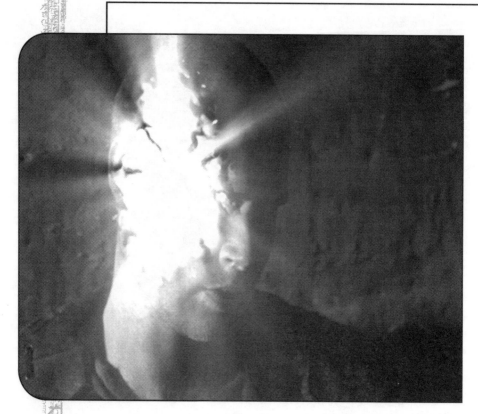

process known as 'mental cleansing' to 'reform' him. The now-docile Durka's arrival aboard Moya was more than Rygel could bear: attempting to assassinate his nemesis with a crudely made bomb, the explosion instead reverses the effects of the Nebari cleansing, restoring Durka to his evil ways.

After killing his Nebari captor, Salis, and attempting to assume command of Moya by holding Aeryn and Rygel hostage, Durka is last seen being ejected into space in the remains of a Nebari transport ship. Rygel, however, fears that he may not have seen the last of his old adversary.

That Durka was a character deemed simply too deliciously evil to stay dead was largely due to the chilling performance of David Wheeler. Primarily a theatre actor, he has appeared in countless Australian stage productions over the past quarter century.

Stark is a member of the Banik slave race, a species able to block their thoughts, even from the terrifying probings of the Peacekeepers' Aurora Chair. This resistance to the supposedly unassailable power of the Chair, even through 100 interrogation sessions, allowed Stark to remain alive for two cycles before Crichton was placed in his cell on the Gammak base. Stark, like all members of his race, is able to share images of things he has seen with others, by removing his mask and revealing a glowing surface that appears to be his true face. This can be a calming experience, and eases the suffering of the sick and dying.

Stark was portrayed by Paul Goddard, an actor also known for his role in another science-fiction production shot in Sydney — he played Agent Brown in *The Matrix*.

Maldis

"I feed on death. But don't we all? Some eat plants, some meat... I consume the life essence itself – preferably medium rare."

Maldis is a cruel and malevolent energy vampire, apparently invincible, who subjugates whole planets in order to feed off their life energy, thriving on fear, pain, hatred and — for the "main course" — death. As well as being able to simply 'wish' things into reality, he can remove a creature's spirit from its body and instantaneously bring it to his lair. There, he will use his ability to 'tune in' to the past histories of his victims, in order to discover their weaknesses and vulnerabilities.

Able to change his physical appearance at will, his preferred manifestation is as a white-haired, yellow-eyed and black-leather clad male. He also is known to use many other names — including IGG, and Haloth — making him extremely difficult to identify. Maldis cannot be harmed by physical attacks; he is only affected by beings with immense spiritual powers. Although he is dispersed by Zhaan's energy burst, she believes that Maldis will coalesce again in time, and that their first encounter will not be their last.

The role of the sorcerer Maldis marked English-born actor Chris Haywood's seventieth film and television credit in a career spanning twenty-five years, which has included such well-known Australian movies as *Breaker Morant* and *Shine*. ∎

THE EFFECTS

"There's life out here, Dad. Weird, amazing, psychotic life. And death, in Technicolor..."

– John Crichton

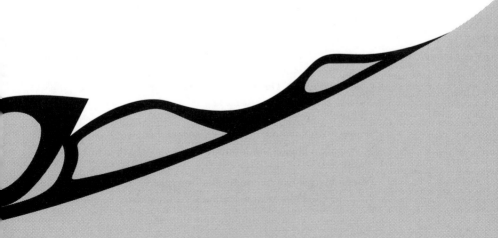

Virginia Hey

"Henson's Creature Shop are all mad scientists with the genius to create characters who are so lifelike, we often forget that numerous people are operating each one. They have almost the same facial movement as a human. It's uncanny."

Jim Henson's Creature Shop has come a long way since the days of *Pigs in Space*. The company founded by legendary puppeteer Jim Henson has constantly pushed the envelope of puppetry, animatronics and special effects, creating ground-breaking television like *The Storyteller*, *Dinosaurs* and *Merlin*, and such astonishingly realised feature films as *The Dark Crystal*, *Labyrinth*, *Teenage Mutant Ninja Turtles*, *The Flintstones* and *Babe*. Most recently, The Jim Henson Company launched *Farscape* into the ratings stratosphere, an extraordinarily ambitious project combining the artistry of the Creature Shop with science-fiction scripts in a way that had never been done before.

"The vision and ambition of *Farscape* was to go where no show had gone before," says Creature Shop special visual-effects supervisor Jamie Courtier, "and bring feature film special effects to a television show. So, the way we built D'Argo, Rygel and Pilot is to the same kind of standard and criteria that would apply to a film." While the Creature Shop had never produced anything quite like *Farscape*, the process by which D'Argo, Scorpius, NamTar, Rygel, Pilot and all other alien species are brought to life is much the same as for any Creature Shop creation. Working from a finalised design sketch, "we produce a maquette," Courtier explains, referring to a small-scale sculpture made from Plastolene — an oil-based clay that never dries out — which, when painted, moulded and cast, becomes the keystone of the character. "If we are going to do CGI work," he adds, "it'll become the scanning maquette as well. Then, having set our target with that little aesthetic model, we start the project."

Such projects, says Courtier, operate on the principle of the inverted pyramid, starting small, with the maquette, and growing larger as soon as the mould-makers become involved and begin the process of scaling the maquette up to life-size: "The mould shop then make an outside jacket, if it's a character like Pilot, then take a case mould, the outside of the sculpt. They then take an inner mould, and those two moulds go together, and when they've stripped the clay away and hollowed the moulds out, the cavity between them is filled with foam latex rubber, which sets to make the skin. The mould shop also makes a core, which is the inside shape, over which the skin fits, and that core goes to the 'mechies' — the engineers or electronic designers who are going to make the thing work." At this point, the

Above: Pilot is one of the most complex animatronic puppets built by the Creature Shop for the show.

pyramid begins to widen. Artists and fabricators set about rebuilding the structure in tough but flexible materials, such as foam latex or lightweight plastics, depending on whether the creature will be 'prosthetic' (worn by an actor or performer) or 'animatronic' (puppets with no strings attached). "Then, it's testing and finishing, rehearsing and commissioning, making sure that everything works," Courtier adds. On a feature film, the whole process can take up to six or seven months from concept to camera. On a quick-turnaround television show, a new creature can be created within weeks.

Often, several versions of a single creature must be built to accommodate the different needs of shooting. "With Rygel, for instance, there were two versions," Courtier reveals, "a radio-controlled one, which was quite a complex puppet; and one 'HOT' puppet, as we call it, which stands for 'Hand Operated Torso'. His ThroneSled was a fairly complex thing to make as well, and so were the pole arms — things around puppets like Rygel, which are weight-support pieces of equipment — because they end up being quite heavy, and the weight can compromise the performance. We try and help that out by all sorts of means — bungee rigs; monopod stands that can be rested on the floor and telescope up and down; pole arms; a whole bunch

of paraphernalia. And in the case of Pilot, you'll have spare arms and 'stunt' arms — wire arms that can be worked by puppeteers."

Although animatronic creatures like Rygel and Pilot, which combine complex electronics with expert puppeteers, are among the most typical job the Creature Shop undertakes, many other *Farscape* species are created by applying prosthetics to actors. "D'Argo is pure prosthetics," Courtier confirms. "There aren't any animatronics involved at all. But one normally thinks of prosthetics as just being facial additions in silicone or foam latex, whereas D'Argo is more complex, with little bits of hard shell on him and a bit of enhancing on top of his head." In fact, D'Argo was originally designed as a combination of animatronics and prosthetics — much like NamTar from 'DNA Mad Scientist' — "but as a key character, I think we felt that it was too much of a burden, because with animatronics — especially if it's prosthetic *and* animatronics that we have to fit to a person — it takes such a long time, and it took a long time to rig up D'Argo anyway. It's a big make-up job." In addition, Courtier says, "animatronics are always susceptible to breakdown, and thereby will slow production down, so it was something that we relieved ourselves of, that particular prospect."

Besides, he adds, "we have enough animatronics on the show already!"

Although the process of creating a prosthetics-based character like D'Argo begins in much the same way as an animatronic creature — with a design sketch and a maquette — the procedure is very different. "With a form-hugging facial prosthetic like D'Argo's," Courtier explains, "we actually need the actor here, as opposed to making an animatronic creature which is performed by puppeteers, and can be delivered and set up and performed by anybody, within reason, around the world." Thus, actor Anthony Simcoe flew to the Creature Shop in London, where he was subjected to a full body cast. "I turned up at Henson's," Simcoe recalls, "and met all these incredible people who gave me a life cast from head to toe. I was basically naked, surrounded by six strangers, and covered in plaster, thinking, 'What have I gotten myself into?'"

According to Courtier, the process of creating a prosthetic-based character still follows the pattern of an inverted pyramid, "but it's narrower — less people are involved, because there's no engineering. In D'Argo's case," he adds, "a very masterful sculptor and make-up person named Nigel Booth sculpted, in Plastolene, the D'Argo that we see on screen, on top of

Left and above:
Anthony Simcoe in
prosthetic make-up.

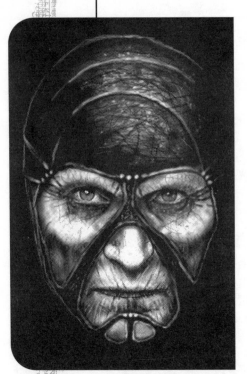

Anthony's life cast. Then we made a mould of that, but rather than making a core mould, Anthony's head was actually the core, so the cavity between his head and the outside case mould, after we stripped away the Plastolene, became the space that we filled with silicone or foam latex."

Of course, unlike an animatronic creature such as Rygel or Pilot, D'Argo, as with all prosthetically-enhanced characters, has to be rebuilt, virtually from scratch, on each day of shooting. That process is the responsibility of Creature Shop creative supervisor Dave Elsey's department, situated on the Sydney set of *Farscape*, 12,000 miles away from the London Creature Shop. "D'Argo's is an incredibly complicated make-up for a television show like this," Elsey asserts. "I can't think of another show that has anything that compares to it. It used to take three hours to get Anthony into it, but it's now down to an hour and a half — and on a good day, he's in it in an hour! But although it's a very complicated make-up," he adds, "it's very well designed, so the only things we replace every single day are his chin piece and his face piece. The rest is reusable — his beard, the head, the tentacles and his chest."

No matter how good a prosthetic may be, however, the responsibility of bringing it to life comes down to the actor wearing it. "Anthony Simcoe just brings it to life fantastically," Elsey states. "He absolutely knows how it works on screen, and how to move around in it to get the best possible movement out of it. Obviously, he knows how his own face works on screen, but D'Argo's face works in a completely different way, so he has to adjust for the make-up." Simcoe agrees. "It's definitely different from working with your own face," he says. "It moves so differently and reads so differently in the lens, especially with D'Argo, because that chin makes his face so elongated. Working out how he moves, and using that within the frame, was a really big learning curve." On the other hand, he adds, "when you look at people's faces, they move a lot less than you think, so we spent a lot of time looking at my face normally, and then my face in the mask, to see how much we had to translate between the two. And I'm still learning all the time about how I can use it effectively."

Of course, with a three-hour make-up every day of shooting, patience is not so much a virtue as a necessity. "He's very, very patient," Elsey says of Simcoe. "Unless you've actually been in make-up that much, it's impossible to visualise what it's like to sit down in the make-up chair and start the process every single day. The only way he gets through it is because he has a fantastic sense of humour. He's a very funny guy." According to Simcoe's co-star, Virginia Hey, who spends an equal amount of time in the make-up chair being transformed into Zhaan, Simcoe has another way of coping with the marathon make-up sessions. "Anthony, lucky duck, can go to sleep," she laughs. "He's got this chair that flips back, and he puts his feet up, and he literally just goes off to sleep." Simcoe admits as much, but demurs: "The make-up takes up to three hours, but I can only sleep for the middle forty minutes — while they're doing the detail stuff around my eyes. I can nod off when they're doing that."

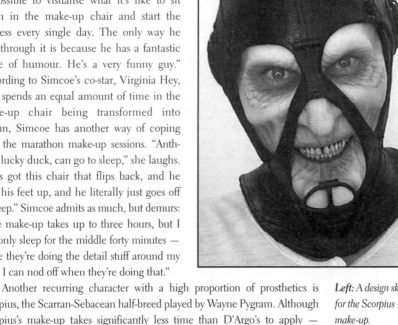

Left: A design sketch for the Scorpius make-up.

Above: Wayne Pygram wearing make-up created from 'Hot Flesh'.

Another recurring character with a high proportion of prosthetics is Scorpius, the Scarran-Sebacean half-breed played by Wayne Pygram. Although Scorpius's make-up takes significantly less time than D'Argo's to apply — around fifty minutes, according to Dave Elsey — the truly remarkable aspect is that it's not made from foam latex, which has been the industry standard for prosthetics for decades. "In the early days of the show, we were using foam latex," Jamie Courtier notes. "Now, the Creature Shop in Sydney, which supports the show on a day-to-day basis, is changing the skin technology to a material called 'Hot Flesh' which is very, very flesh-like."

Elsey, who invented the innovative new material with colleague Colin Ware, describes its origin. "Before we started working on *Farscape*, Colin and I had been messing around with translucent appliances for a long time, because foam latex is opaque, and therefore requires a lot of skill and artwork to make it appear like skin. Skin is translucent — light can penetrate it, and blood can be seen through it — for that reason, foam latex is usually pretty disappointing close up. So, we were experimenting with translucency, and we went through all the gelatins, and eventually we put a bunch of materials together and found we had literally invented this thing we called Hot Flesh. We used it for the first time a week before Scorpius was due to arrive

on set, and although we only had a week to design and build him, we said, 'Look, we think this is going to work, but we're not 100 per cent sure,' and we went all-out and pursued it. Right up until the day that we stuck it on Wayne, we didn't know if it was going to go together or not." Luckily, it did, and to great effect.

"It's the most incredible stuff," Elsey enthuses, listing its advantages: "It has 3,000 per cent elongation, which means I can grab an inch and stretch it to three or four feet. It's reusable, which means it's eco-friendly, as opposed to foam latex, which you use once and throw away. It's translucent, it takes all of the make-up material that we normally use, and it's completely safe. It's also absolutely maintenance-free — we stick Wayne in it in the morning, and we really don't have to do too much to him all day, whereas with other make-ups it's pretty much patch-patch-patch all day long." In fact, Hot Flesh's only disadvantage is it has slightly more density than foam latex, and is therefore heavier. Nevertheless, says Elsey, "Wayne Pygram says it's incredible to wear. It really looks and feels exactly like skin, so when he's got it on, he doesn't actually feel like he's wearing make-up, and if he touches his face, there's no sensation of actually having anything on there, other than the fact that he feels a bit numb. We're still doing foam latex make-ups, but only because we haven't got enough Hot Flesh to go around yet."

Although D'Argo and Scorpius both involve extremely complex prosthetic make-ups, even more complicated actor-based creations have sprung from individual episodes. *Farscape* is replete with such creatures — the Tavleks, Ilanics, Sheyangs, Vorcarian Blood Trackers, *et al* — but no single character has proven quite so challenging to the Creature Shop creatives as NamTar, the extraordinary title character from the episode 'DNA Mad Scientist'. In a misguided quest to transform himself through genetic experimentation into his idea of a perfect life form, no matter what the cost to others, the softly-spoken NamTar's appearance — either grotesquely misshapen or eerily beautiful, depending on your aesthetic — remains one of the Creature Shop's finest moments, even if he does look like something out of a fetish magazine. "He was, partly," laughs Dave Elsey, NamTar's designer.

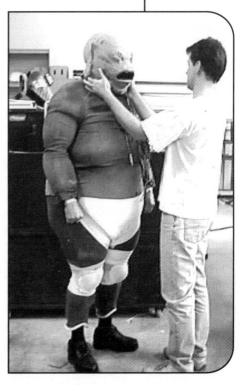

According to Elsey, NamTar's creation evolved like any other *Farscape* species. "The writers usually don't describe the creature," he points out. "They normally leave that open, to a certain extent. But what they do say is what they want the creature to be able to do, and that's the angle from which we come at it, and decide whether it's a make-up, or a puppet, or a guy in a mask or something like that." After discussing ideas with the writers, Elsey spends half a day sketching by hand or on the computer, producing an accurate colour rendering of the creature which he can then show to them: "Nine times out of ten, they'll say 'Yeah, that's exactly it,' so then I show it to the director and the producers, and when I've got the go-ahead from everybody, I start screaming for them to cast the role as fast as possible, so I can get them into a body cast."

Left and above: Sheyangs under construction in the Sydney Creature Shop.

Thus, with NamTar, Elsey and his team had a broad outline of the creature's nature, but an open brief with regard to his actual look. "We wanted to create a really good villain," he says, "and I also wanted to do something different, because I was starting to feel like everything was having too human a shape, and that always worries me." Elsey naturally took the fact that 'NamTar' was 'Rat Man' written backwards as a starting point — hence the mouse ears and rat features — but it was the creature's double-jointed legs which were the true flash of inspiration. "A few years before, we'd built

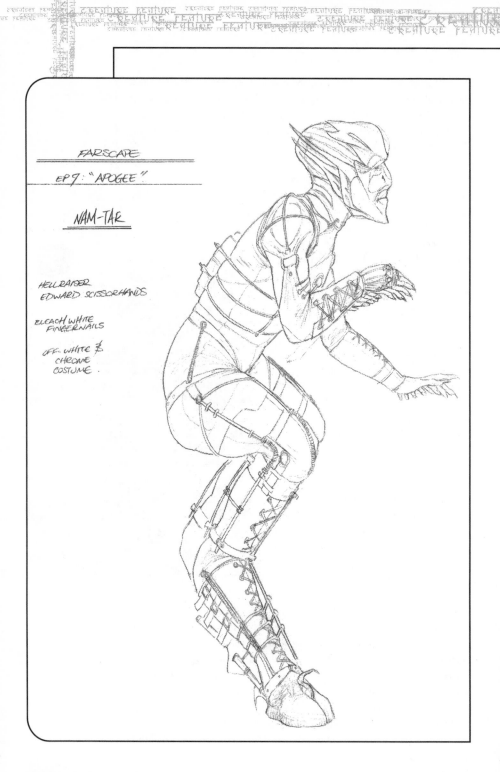

FARSCAPE

EP 9 : "APOGEE"

NAM-TAR

HELLRAISER
EDWARD SCISSORHANDS

BLEACH WHITE
FINGERNAILS

OFF. WHITE &
CHROME
COSTUME.

these things called 'leg extensions', which make somebody's legs look like dog-legs at the back, by giving them that extra joint. We built them for a Nike commercial in which all these footballers are playing football with the devil, and quite by surprise we discovered that the guy who ended up wearing the NamTar costume — Adrian Getley, who was on our crew — could actually walk around in the extensions, even though they'd originally been made just to stand still in. I remembered this, so we rebuilt them, and made some improvements, like putting in some shock absorbers so you could walk around on concrete, and when we showed everybody they all went, 'Wow, I've never seen anything like that before!'"

Having worked out NamTar's legs, Elsey says, the rest of the character came together easily. "He had a mechanical face," he adds, "but we had to use the actor's own eyes, because he had to be able to see where he was going in those leg extensions, so we used contact lenses." With the addition of voice actor Julian Garner's dulcet tones, NamTar was born. "That was a really great one to do," Elsey says proudly. "I remember looking around the set at NamTar, and Kornata, his deformed assistant, and saying to Adrian, 'Look at all this rubber!' And he said, 'What about D'Argo, and Zhaan's ears?' And I'd sort of forgotten about the main cast... because you get used to them!"

One of the last original creations from the first series appeared in the penultimate episode, 'Bone to be Wild', in which Ben Browder's real-life

Left: Initial design sketch for NamTar.

Above: An early stage of M'Lee from 'Bone to be Wild'.

wife, Francesca Buller, played the calciferous creature M'Lee. "That was another thing we actually used Hot Flesh on," Elsey explains. "All of those weird spiky things on the back of her head were made of Hot Flesh, and they were all mechanical, so they could stretch on cue. So, when she transforms from good M'Lee into evil M'Lee, you can do the complete transformation in one take. Cool! She also had lights in her head which showed her mood, because we're always trying to think of interesting angles. Everything we do is basically script-led," he adds, "so we will do whatever we think is right for the script. If that's just a pair of contact lenses or two fangs or a nose tip, fine — we'll do that, and we won't feel bad about doing that because I think you have to have just as much skill to do that properly as anything else. But, at the same time, we never shy away from doing the more complicated stuff, either. Most of the time we try to keep everything as alien as we possibly can."

Sometimes, of course, this means avoiding the 'man in a suit' approach — something which, having started out with hand-operated and rod-operated puppets, the Creature Shop is uniquely qualified to do. One of Dave Elsey's first tasks on *Farscape* was, in fact, to create such a creature: the alien Proprietor of a commerce planet visited by Crichton and company during the first episode. As Elsey recalls of those early days: "I went to a meeting, and they started talking about the characters going to this commerce planet, and I said, 'Excuse me, what are the people like on the commerce planet?' And they said, 'Well, they're all aliens, obviously.' And I was like, 'Oh my God! I've got to build the whole bloody universe in three weeks!'"

Elsey, who had recently arrived in Sydney from England to start work on *Farscape*'s first episodes, immediately began breaking open boxes shipped from the London Creature Shop, but found only the elements required for the main characters: D'Argo, Zhaan, Rygel and Pilot. "I thought, 'Oh no, I've got to build everything else for the show, and of course every episode they land on a different planet, and every planet they land on has these aliens on it!'" Operating from a makeshift workshop — "a converted car park with a table in it" — Elsey began gathering the materials he would need, but soon discovered that everything was different Down Under: "I found that none of the materials were called the same thing, they all had different code numbers, they all worked differently, the setting times for everything was different, the humidity affected the foam latex differently... Basically, nothing was what I expected it to be, and nothing worked the way I wanted it to, so I was exactly like John Crichton — in the middle of this alien world, not knowing how anything worked any more! Nothing I'd learned could really prepare me for it."

The first order of business, however, was the Proprietor. "There was a whole bunch of sketches for it when I arrived, some of which were really good," Elsey recalls. "We kind of rejected all of them except for one version of it, which was only a picture of the head, so I did a really quick sketch of the rest of the body. Then we worked out how we were going to fit people into it and make it work, which is half of the job — not just working out what it looks like, but how you're going to get it to operate." Elsey figured that the Proprietor would need three people inside it to make it work, and that the main problem would be hiding them from view. "By this time, we had a week to build this thing, which was eight-foot-high by six-foot-wide in every direction. It was a bit of a nightmare," he admits, "but we worked like devils and we got it all done. Having worked all night the night before they were due to start shooting, we went straight on set with it, without actually going to bed." The worst was yet to come, however.

"The puppeteers climbed into it, and the whole thing pitched forward and fell flat on its face, with all the puppeteers inside it! None of us reacted," Elsey remembers. "All of the people who'd been up all night just

Above: The huge Proprietor was operated from the inside by a team of three puppeteers.

stood there with their mouths open, while the puppeteers crawled out of every orifice. Then we calmly went over and picked it up and dusted off the face, and tried a few levers and it all still worked."

Despite these initial setbacks, Elsey says that, after the first season's opening episodes, the show started to run "like clockwork," even though the nature of series television means that there is constant time pressure. "Apart from the main characters, which need continual updating, and the new stuff we have to build all the time, there's what we call the 'gags' — people being shot, or lit on fire, or being cut in half, or having their eyes removed, or their arm dissolved..." Then there are the 'throwaway' items — such as the tiny two-headed Trelkez from 'That Old Black Magic' — which may be on screen for a few seconds but can often take two weeks to build. "I reckon the shortest amount of time we can do anything at all is a week, and that'll be a make-up, because we can't even think about doing anything animatronic in that time. That's what the show's like all the time," Elsey adds, in a way which suggests that the time pressures are something that he and his team relish — at least, in retrospect. "It's such a fast turnover," he says, "whatever we're building, we get it done just in time, we get it on set, and usually the first thing that happens is that they'll dump it in water, or stick mud all over it, or shoot it to bits! But that's just the way *Farscape* is. I was a bit shell-shocked when I arrived, but I'm completely used to it now."

In fact, Elsey describes himself as "the world's biggest *Farscape* fan. I feel like I really know the show, and I have a big say in the way things look and the way things are done. I've even had influence over some of the stories at times, and that's something that I've never had before. I'm a big fan of science fiction and horror, anything with something unusual in it, and I think that the biggest strength that *Farscape* has over all those other shows is that Crichton's constantly surprised by where he finds himself and what he's looking at. When he meets aliens, he's the first one to go, 'Wow, look at that! What do you call that?' He's had to adjust his attitude,

because he's like somebody looking at animals in a zoo, and then finds out that the animals actually have personalities and can talk back!

"I really like the fact that *Farscape* is a very alien show, so that everything is weird and bizarre, apart from Crichton. On *Star Trek*, for example, the humans are the ones in charge, but on *Farscape*, Crichton has no idea what's going on most of the time, and nobody has any respect for him whatsoever. So he's really the underdog, and I like that. They also take chances with characters that they don't normally do with other shows, particularly with science fiction. You'd think that sci-fi, being an imaginative thing, would take chances, but most sci-fi shows are very conservative and safe, and there are lots of rules that go along with them. *Farscape* throws those away. The characters are seriously flawed — they've got some seriously messed-up aliens who weren't picked up enough as children! I would watch the show, even if I didn't work on it, because I like shows that have wacky aliens in it that are surprising, not just guys wearing prosthetic foreheads. Everyone's seen so many movies that have incredible aliens and creatures in them, and I really think people watching television want the same kind of thing, and that's what we're trying to give them."

Left: Though seen only briefly, the Trelkez is a fully realised creation.

Above: One of the many 'background creatures' designed by Dave Elsey for the series.

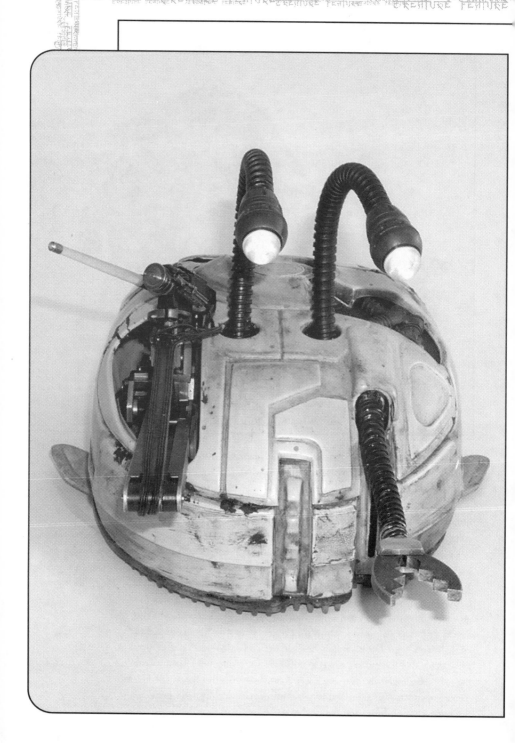

Of course, not all of the ideas spawned by the numerous creative elements of *Farscape* reach the screen. For example, at one point in the early development stages of the show, then known as *Space Chase*, the cast of regular characters included a robot. "I would love to have done that," says Jamie Courtier, "because like R2-D2 and C-3PO, the prospect of creating a robot character is always enchanting. We did it for the *Lost in Space* movie, but that wasn't really a great character in the way that a *Farscape* robot would have been. The robot that we were going to build had a lot of humour, and would have been quite a comic character, I think." However, the Creature Shop did get to create a kind of robot — the Diagnostic Repair Drones, known as DRDs.

"We very much enjoyed building them," Courtier says, "because they were a technical challenge. A lot of the creatures we've got have skins, and there's an artistry and a whole set of criteria that goes along with producing things with skins on them, but the downside is that they're quite high maintenance — they deteriorate with time, so you've got to repair and re-paint them. But when you are making a little machine, or even a big one, it's just kind of there. It's a piece of hardware, like an espresso machine in the kitchen — it just stays there for quite a long time without any problems." Courtier says that half a dozen DRDs were built, to different specifications depending on the usage: "The DRDs were both radio-controlled and puppets, hand-operated from underneath the set for the close-up work. Some of them were 'gofers' which you'd see running down the corridor, just like little remote control cars. And then there were more complex animatronic ones, which have stuff popping out of them — arms and scopes and all the rest of it. Those were basically upgrades from the hand puppets, so you could actually do more dextrous tasks with them, like operate the pliers to pick things up. They're constantly being amended and customised for various episodes."

With radio-controlled robots, animatronic creatures, prosthetic appliances and creatures which are combinations of all three, the Creature Shop has come a long way since the days of glove puppets like Kermit the Frog. And yet, as Jamie Courtier points out, most people still think that the work of Jim Henson's Creature Shop is mainly about Muppets. "Obviously, we take every chance we can to dispel that myth," he says, "because we work on technologically complex, computer-controlled hydraulic creatures just as much as we work on simple rod puppets. You can't pigeonhole the Creature Shop."

Dave Elsey is equally enthusiastic about his role on the show: "One day we'll be doing a hand puppet, the next day we'll be doing a full-size rod puppet, then something the size of your hand, then we'll be doing a make-up on someone, or a creation that's half-mechanical and half-make-up... I get to work on everything that I've ever thought of doing in my entire life — and a few things that I've never thought of as well!" ■

Matt Carroll

"Farscape is one of those shows that's fantastic for people to work on because you are using every particular type of visual effect."

he biggest changes to hit the film industry in the past twenty-five years have undoubtedly occurred in the field of special effects. Computer generated imagery (CGI) has transformed the world of film and television, yet it's less than twenty years since audiences were amazed by the Genesis Project simulation sequence in *Star Trek II: The Wrath of Khan*. As Ben Browder proudly proclaims, there are more CG shots in the première episode of *Farscape* than in all of *Independence Day*, the movie so highly acclaimed for its special effects made just three years earlier.

There's a danger involved with CGI, however. The effects can become the driving force, covering up a weak script and poor production. The creators of *Farscape* knew from day one that they wanted to combine the different fields of special effects to tell their story, but it would always be the story that took precedence.

With the Creature Shop covering their own field of expertise, executive producer and series creator Rockne S. O'Bannon and producer Matt Carroll had to find people equally capable of dealing with the visual effects. Accordingly, a pitching process was set up. Six of the leading effects houses in Australia were invited to show the producers what they could do. British-born Paul Butterworth was hired by Garner McLellan Design in Sydney to assist them with their presentation. Garner McLellan was, up to that point, a visual-effects house for commercials and interactive designs, but now wanted to expand into television episodes and feature films. Butterworth's initial task was to prepare three one-off images, or style frames, which would evoke the mood he thought the show needed.

"I essentially had three scripts at the start," he recalls. "One was a script that never actually saw the light of day, about this sort of slime monster that was on a battleship — it was like a cross between a cool battle cruiser and a ghost ship. So I painted up a ghost ship frame alongside one of the CG creative directors, Andrew Helland. We then designed an early *Farscape 1* module that was being launched above Earth's atmosphere; and thirdly had an early design of Moya floating through the clouds of an alien planet.

"I painted them in a very filmic way: I adopted a widescreen format. They had a really good filmic feel to them, and I think a lot of the strength of where we went as a creative team was based on those style frames. We were trying to make *Star Wars* for television. The initial ethos was to create a colour and light and mood for the series that was different.

We looked at *Alien*, and really liked the whole blackness of that, but had to make *Farscape* a little bit more adventurous."

The producers were impressed enough by the presentation for Garner McLellan to be awarded the job. "They came from a very creative standpoint," says Pete Coogan, production executive for The Jim Henson Company. "We told them what the budget was, and what we wanted to do. They were in commercials and opening title sequences, and they saw this as entry to long-form. The attention to detail of their designers was second to none; it just blew us away."

Naturally, some problems needed to be sorted out. "Essentially you had a group of television people, who did long-form, and had never really done this sort of exacting science that we did," Paul Butterworth explains. "We always had very high ideals about what we wanted to do, and obviously those had to be squeezed into the show's time frame. So, there were two very different cultures. It was definitely an uneasy marriage at the start, when we had to work out what to call things, and educate each other on how to develop the process. It had never been done in Australia, and no one on the show had done this sort of scale of visual effects before for a TV series."

Above: This shot of the Commerce planet in the première episode is an impressive example of Garner McLellan's work.

Work was required on two main elements: three-dimensional images, such as spaceships and planets, which had to be seen moving, and two-dimensional images, such as matte paintings, used to enhance the set or provide backdrops for scenes. A team was quickly selected for the task. "The *Farscape* visual-effects team was about thirty people," Garner McLellan's line producer Jason Bath says. "Paul was the visual-effects director, and he led overall the creative side — the look and feel to it — very much in conjunction with Andrew Hill and Steve James, who were the creative heads of the 3D department. We had two full-time compositors, and then we had a 3D crew, and also a compositing crew working on 2D workstations. At first it was tough, because everybody on the production was a little inexperienced, and so just the sheer number of shots really swamped us. By the time we got through to about episode ten, we'd worked out the best models and the best pathways to achieve things, where we used the shots more cleverly in the episodes. We struck a balance and really hit our stride after episode ten. Our systems were working, and the feedback with editing and production was working as well."

The production team devised a system so that directors didn't overload the CG house with unreasonable demands. "Every director had a package of

what they could achieve," Matt Carroll recalls. "They had what we called 'credit cards', in terms of what they could do with visual effects. So, when the director got the script, he would sit down with the visual-effects house and he had a number of 'tokens' which he could use up. The visual-effects team could only output a certain amount of work, so if you went for three big shots, what we call A-shots, then you couldn't have a lot of smaller C-shots. We divided them all into ones and twos as well. C2s were simple CG shots: just laser fire, for example. So you could trade; say, a big A2 shot for fifteen C2 shots. If you had a big visual effect, like a fire fight with lots of laser shooting, then you couldn't afford to have a matte painting. That was sometimes very hard to juggle, because you were always trying to go down onto some alien place, and the only way you could establish that was through matte paintings or set extensions."

"An A-shot is a more complex shot that involves both 3D animation and 2D work," Jason Bath adds. "An A1 is a serious shot involving a moving camera and probably complex matte paintings. A B-shot can involve both 3D and 2D elements, but it involves no other action, so we didn't have to wait for the shooting of any live-action material for a B-shot. Those are the

Left and above: Two examples of C-shots: a hologram and laser fire.

ones we got onto first. As soon as we discussed the script with the director, we could go straight ahead with the B-shots. Things like Moya flying through space in front of a planet, or the *Farscape 1* module. All those sorts of 'in space' things that didn't need any live action. The C-shots are those that only have 2D effects overlaid on them: gunfire, for example, or a hologram. Once we'd worked ourselves up a recipe for these shots, we could turn them out very quickly. So we were able to offer a lot of C-shots and be quite flexible. If there was a gun battle and you knew they wanted twenty-five C-shots instead of the allowed fifteen, we could often very easily accommodate that."

Once Garner McLellan began work, they became intricately involved with other parts of the production process. "The majority of our co-ordination was with editing and with the episode director," Jason Bath explains. "There was a supervising director for the series, Andrew Prowse, who was fantastic because he cast an overall eye and was able to brief us on the visual effects, and give us approvals. We'd submit a rough animation to editing just for timing and action; they could drop that into the cuts and see how it was working. We could bounce it back and forwards like that, then once we locked it off we could go ahead and do different versions. Obviously there were also some supervision requirements on set for the complicated shots. I would liaise with the production and get Paul or one of our senior people to supervise anything like that."

Left: The computer-generated Rygel rises to the occasion in 'Jeremiah Crichton'.

Butterworth's presence was needed on set during the filming of D'Argo's fall from Moya in 'They've Got a Secret'. Anthony Simcoe was placed on a piece of apparatus called a gimbal, so that he could be photographed from every angle, as if he was in freewheel motion. "I worked up a pre-visualisation of what D'Argo would see going down the tunnel," Butterworth recalls, "and that was played back on the day in front of Anthony while he was on the gimbal, so he could have a reaction to it. His actions were thrown into the 3D scene and then we built the whole tunnel that D'Argo was laid into."

Every episode presented new challenges for the visual-effects team. "I tried to push it as far as possible," Butterworth maintains. "We were always trying very new techniques with the development of matte paintings: we'd project matte paintings onto 3D shapes so they wouldn't be flat, and you could actually move round them to a certain degree. We developed a lot of stuff like nebula clouds and particles; they're really expensive from a rendering point of view.

"Every time you came back to Moya or to another planet, I liked to try and turn the camera to a different angle. One thing that really bored me with a lot of the other sci-fi shows was the fact that they always approach the camera shots from a flat plane. Space is all about three dimensionality, and so in 'Throne for a Loss' we actually opened up with Moya at right angles to us, really tight in. We were going to show Moya a lot of times over the entire show, so it was good to keep on showing different aspects, and trying to get across the sense of scale. It is really hard when you've got a three-kilometre-long ship in the middle of space — it's difficult to give reference to its size each time."

CGI also helped out when circumstances prevented a Creature Shop puppet from being used — notably in the episode 'Jeremiah Crichton', in which Rygel had to float above a crowd of adoring Acquarans. A 3D, CG Rygel made his début in 'Exodus From Genesis', hiding from the gestating Queen, but 'Jeremiah Crichton' was his big episode. "3D Rygel was quite a beast in itself," Butterworth remembers. "All his animation was predominantly handled by Graham Binding. He had to match the real, live-action Rygel, and that had its complications — he kept on changing costumes! Over time Rygel has evolved: every time they made a different puppet it would be painted slightly differently, so whenever we did a CG Rygel, he had to be re-tweaked and re-matched to the live-action one."

Sydney Creature Shop supervisor Dave Elsey pays tribute to the CG artists: "The CG department work hand-in-hand with us, and the CG on the show is incredible. We help each other out an awful lot, and because of that we're able to accomplish much, much bigger things." ■

STARBURST

One of the most frequently seen CG shots in *Farscape* is Moya's entry into Star-
Burst. Paul Butterworth explains how this was achieved: "The StarBurst
was discussed *ad infinitum*, and everyone had their own ideas of what it
would look like. Brian Henson described it as essentially a tear in space
that opened up. So I did a couple of key paintings based on the wires or
lines across the body of the ship. I wanted the actual Moya
pattern, all the tattoo-like lines and circles and dots that I masked onto the
skin of the ship, to be just like star charts. Energy lights up these power
lines, and a succession of fields of energy run across the ship towards the
front of the body. As that energy races along the body, so the arms of Moya
open up, and create an energy loop at the back. That energy loop then
slides across the body to be in front of the ship, and Moya sort of
races through.

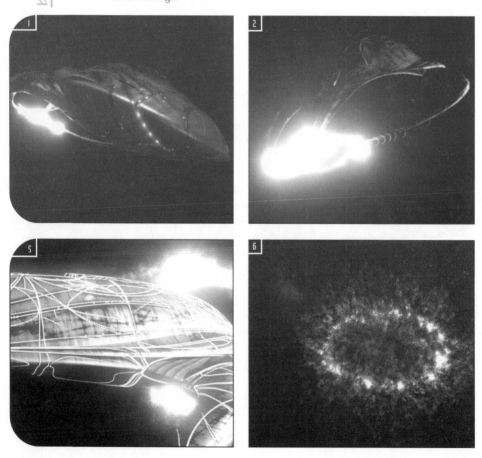

"We made a whole load of animating maps that ran across the body, and there was a skin made up that showed the energy lines, that was hand animated and then projected onto the body of Moya. That did a lot of reveals of energy across the body. The actual energy loop, or the lining loop, was a series of particles that one of the animators specialised in. She came up with this whole lightning energy look, like energy rings. The assembly of the shots was all handled by Richard Lambert, who became the 'StarBurst King'. He then put it together and did his own sort of special form of magic, and the shots were there.

"The design of StarBurst took a day for me, after we had had a lot of conversations about it. Once I'd painted up the style frames, the actual construction was about six weeks initially, then to render all the elements was about three days. Assembling for Richard was about a week the first time around, and then from that moment on it was a week's turnaround for a StarBurst." ∎

Left and below: StarBurst, from start to finish.

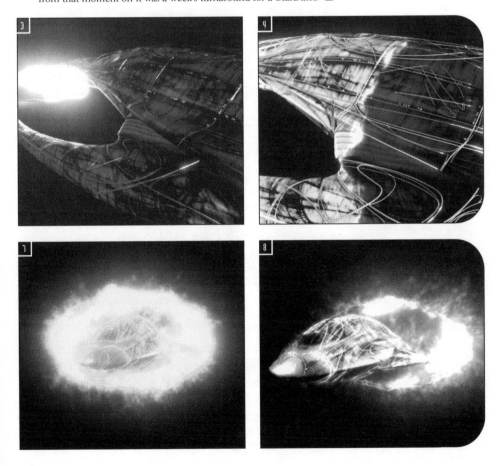

INTO SEASON TWO

Rockne S. O'Bannon

"The last four episodes of season one set an awfully high standard for the series, one which we were determined to match and even surpass in season two."

With a show like *Farscape*, a long time can pass between filming an episode and its appearance on screen. As the first season's early episodes made their way through postproduction, the show's producers, cast and crew couldn't help but wonder: would *Farscape* be the success that everyone involved dared hoped for? A resounding 'Yes!' was the answer. Premièring on the SCI FI Channel in March, 1999, the first season of *Farscape* eventually built a loyal audience in America, before later winging its way across the Atlantic to the BBC, where similarly devoted fans were found.

In August 1999, Claudia Black made a barnstorming appearance in California at the San Diego Comic Convention and was overwhelmed at the enthusiastic reception from the fans. Press reaction was similarly effusive: hailed by national paper *USA Today* as the best reason to subscribe to the SCI FI Channel, and as "a weekly jolt of imagination overload" by the *New York Times*, the show was also rated the "best sci-fi series on television" by *TV Guide*. Further recognition came when the first season was nominated for several prestigious Saturn Awards from the Academy of Science Fiction, Fantasy and Horror Films: Best Syndicated TV series; Best Actor (Ben Browder); Best Actress (Claudia Black); and Best Supporting Actress (Virginia Hey).

The reaction in Britain was equally gratifying. "A new science-fiction series dawns," wrote *Time Out*, previewing the première episode in late November 1999, "bridging the gap between cult and mainstream status, with its tongue edging towards its cheek, and sky-high production values." Meanwhile, the top-selling TV and radio-listings magazine *Radio Times* compared the show favourably with *Star Wars* creator George Lucas's recent output: "Looking at *Farscape*'s breathless blurring of computerised effects, puppets, action and humour, I'd say Lucas has some catching up to do."

Science-fiction magazines began to focus on the series, with *Dream Watch*, *SFX* and *Starburst* in Britain, and *Starlog*, *Cinescape* and *Sci-Fi Universe* in America among the publications devoting major features to the show as its popularity steadily increased. In America, the SCI FI Channel scheduled 'Chain Reaction' nights of back-to-back *Farscape* episodes chosen by the fans, while in Britain, the BBC added a weekly repeat showing to capitalise on the series' quickly growing audience. In the UK, Contender Video released the first season on both video and

extras-laden DVDs, featuring the full-length, forty-eight minute versions of each episode (including numerous extra sequences unseen on television in either Britain or America). An American video and DVD release of the first season was soon announced, along with *Farscape* trading cards, novels and action figures.

Meanwhile, Scapers (as *Farscape* fans call themselves) have quickly become a huge presence on the Internet, with over 100 websites springing up, complementing the show's official site at www.farscape.com. "As long as we keep the science-fiction audience happy," Claudia Black comments on the fan reaction, "which essentially is a very literate and intelligent audience, then somebody is doing a good job."

In this interactive age, the audience's reaction is often immediate, and the website and bulletin boards of both the SCI FI Channel and the BBC were inundated with comments from fans as soon as each episode aired. Discussions about the characters have become quite spirited as viewers each defend their favourites, and it's interesting to note how the fans' opinions have developed over the season.

"Rygel boring? Really?" wrote Nicky Wan on the BBC's bulletin board soon after 'Nerve' aired in Britain. "I think he's one of the most entertaining characters on the show, though I just found him plain annoying at first. He's a scheming, conniving, self-centred little Hynerian, but there's more to him than that, as we've seen throughout the series. At first, like nearly everyone else, I thought D'Argo was a bit of a Klingon clone... but again, as the season's progressed, he's become less 2D and became another interesting member of the crew."

"Rygel's more *annoying* than boring," Ross Marnie posted around the same time, "and I always find it really funny when John calls him 'Sparky.' D'Argo's pretty useful too, as an aggressive but likeable type. Aeryn's simply wonderful and Chiana is so weird she's great. She reminds me of a spider. Something to do with the strange posture she has..."

"I don't think D'Argo's boring at all," added Alan Woodward. "He was instrumental in getting John through the wormhole to the false Earth (in 'A Human Reaction'). He's a dangerous individual who's also unpredictable. He has his compassionate side, though it's somewhat hidden from the others."

Opposite page: The cast head into season two.

Above: *One of the striking computer desktop images available for fans to download from the official Farscape website.*

So where can *Farscape* go next? Perhaps that's the wrong question, since, as executive producer David Kemper points out, there's nowhere that *Farscape can't* go. Even as the first season was building viewers in America, a second batch of twenty-two episodes was going before the cameras in Sydney. "At the beginning of season two, we wanted to build on what we'd started," Andrew Prowse, director and associate producer, recalls, "just consolidate and continue to make strong shows."

Series creator Rockne S. O'Bannon has always believed in the show's potential, and feels that the climax of the first season simply marks the end of the beginning. "In the course of the first year, it was particularly gratifying to see each of the characters taking their first steps on journeys that are uniquely their own," he remarks. "There was great emotional stuff that first year — thanks to an incredible symbiosis of writing, acting and directing. In particular, I enjoyed watching John Crichton beginning his journey from Everyman to hero. In my mind he is destined for mythic stature, and to see him beginning to fit into this strange, strange world, and beginning to assume that mythic role, was extremely exciting. I was able to see that the potential breadth I'd always hoped for the saga was actually possible. That first year was exhausting, yes — but also a thrilling experience. When it was finished, I could tell then that there would be no limits."

"By the time you get to season two," Ben Browder says, "the characters are really beginning to learn from each other. It seems fairly obvious at times that Crichton has had an influence on the others, particularly on Aeryn and D'Argo, though Rygel seems immune to Crichton's influence! D'Argo has become Crichton's friend, his buddy, his rock. Crichton looks to D'Argo for approval and advice on a lot of things."

Claudia Black feels that the addition of Chiana towards the end of the first season provides a lot of potential for season two: "Chiana's a contemporary character who's fascinating. She does exactly as she wishes. She's younger, but wiser than Aeryn. One of the more unusual aspects of *Farscape* is that three of the lead characters are female. What's missing is a female friendship, and I hope that will be between Chiana and Aeryn. There's a tomboy element, and a younger sister/older sister paradigm."

Anthony Simcoe enjoys the prospect of finding out more about the races who populate the *Farscape* universe. "It's nice to fill out the mythology of all the races, whether they're Luxans or Hynerians or whatever," he says. "It's good to move into those worlds and find out a little more about them."

At the close of the first season, Crichton and D'Argo are floating in space, the Luxan drifting into unconsciousness as the Gammak base and its oil-covered moon burn behind them. Aeryn, in her Prowler, is desperately trying to find them, while Scorpius remains obsessed with capturing Crichton for information on wormhole technology. Moya's recently born

baby, Talyn, is under Crais's control, as the former Peacekeeper Captain heads off with him into the unknown. Reluctantly, Moya has StarBursted away, carrying the other three members of Crichton's dysfunctional family — Zhaan, Chiana and Rygel.

Above: Concept art for a female Luxan who is featured in an early season two episode.

The opening episode of the second season contains numerous surprises, as some of the cast are reunited and new alliances are forged. As a result of experiences we learn about later, Zhaan makes some unexpected life choices which come as a relief to her friends, while baby Talyn displays what may prove to be a serious lack of judgement.

Judgement, or the lack of it, is a key theme in the early part of the second season, as Moya's crew continue to be tested under unusual circumstances — a tragedy leads Chiana to steal Aeryn's Prowler and flee from the ship; D'Argo encounters a fellow Luxan who wants him to help her die; an old foe from the first season returns; and some devastating truths about Aeryn's past life as a Peacekeeper come back to haunt her.

"One of the things I'm very proud of," O'Bannon concludes, "is the fact that *Farscape* really is evolving very quickly. It keeps moving, and the audiences who catch and hold on really appreciate that." ■

The *Farscape* universe is as rich and complex linguistically as it is visually. Here's an A-Z guide to a selection of the dag-yo language used in the series, so you don't mix up your eema with your mivonks.

Altex — Hynerian bodily organ

Ammiox — tool used to alleviate Moya's amnexus problems

Amnexus — part of Moya's internal systems

Arn — unit of time roughly equivalent to one Earth hour

Aurora Chair — experimental torture device used by Scorpius to interrogate prisoners, which projects their memories onto a screen

Barkan — Hynerian animal analogous to a bat, as in: He blasted out of there like a barkan out of Hezmana!

Bassim oil — a possession of Zhaan's that Chiana snurches

Blotching — mild expletive used by Furlow, the engineer at Dam-Ba-Da depot: Twice as blotching long as it would if you weren't here.

Bonosphere — outer layer of the atmosphere on Furlow's planet

Cholian curd salad — Hynerian delicacy

Contala tea — a Luxan drink

Crank — mild Zenetan expletive: They blasted the crank out of me!

Cycle — unit of time roughly equivalent to one Earth year

Dag-yo — Nebari term for cool, a word the translator microbes can't cope with

Das-trak krjtor — Scarran expletive

Dench — unit of measurement: I want a three point grid search of every square dench of this asteroid.

Draz — mild Nebari expletive: We can StarBurst the draz out of here!

Dren — universal term for rubbish (sometimes used in a stronger form): All this analysis dren comes really naturally to you.

Eema — Luxan equivalent of backside, as in when D'Argo tells Chiana: You are a real pain in the eema!

Fahrbot — Hynerian word for insanity, as in: You're not just fahrbot, you're magra-fahrbot!

Fellip — creature on Tarsis from whom nectar is taken to make an alcoholic drink

Fillgran — a Delvian plant

Frangle — an engine part (possibly non-existent, since Furlow is trying to bamboozle Crichton when she says it)

Frell — Sebacean expletive, as in: What the frell is causing that magnetic anomaly?

Frotash — type of Luxan garden which D'Argo would like to plant

Gah — Nebari expletive

Glarion frost point — a very low temperature

Greebols — Nebari term for a fool: Why do I always get stuck with the greebols that don't have any plan?

Grezz — another possibly non-existent engine part; see Frangle

Gris — Nebari term similar to dren, as in: We beat the gris out of them!

Grolack — a feast item

Grotless — Nebari term for 'out of my wits': I'm scared grotless!

Hentas — Hynerian unit of short measurement: A bomb, mere hentas from where I was...

Hepatian minced stew — a feast item

Hetch drive — the engine put in *Farscape 1* after Crichton burns off the last of the fuel

Hezmana — Luxan term for hell: Where in the hezmana is that siren coming from?

Jelifan fire paste — an explosive

Jinka poles — Sebacean term, as in: You damage the captain's prize and he'll have both your heads on jinka poles!

Juka — expletive used by the botanist Br'Nee

Juxt — mild Hynerian expletive: What the juxt was that?!

Kal tanega, chivoko — Sebacean phrase roughly translated as 'a crowning glory'

Karjik Pulse — form of tracking device used by the Peacekeepers, attuned to energy sources

Krawldar — Hynerian delicacy

Kronite — remnants of past Peacekeeper cargo which have explosive properties

Lerg — Sebacean number as in: Level four, number six lerg five.

Living Death — Sebacean name for an irreversible comatose state induced by exposure to high temperatures

Lutra oil — a volatile explosive

Marauder — Peacekeeper assault ship

Marjols — a delicacy enjoyed by Hynerians

Masata — Acquaran term for saviour

Mellet — something that is not very pleasant served chopped

Microt — unit of time roughly equivalent to one Earth second

Mivonks — intimate male body part, as in: She's clearly leading D'Argo around by his mivonks.

Nerfer — Sebacean term for someone who plays by-the-book: Guess he's not as big a nerfer as I thought he was.

Numnas — derogative Sebacean expression for guts, as in: You haven't got the numnas to go through with this!

Panthak jab — a type of blow used by Peacekeepers in battle to knock out a foe

Paraphoral nerve — part of the Sebacean anatomy which facilitates the removal of toxins from the body, but does not regenerate when damaged. (This is similar to the function of the liver in the human body.)

Pedrark — Luxan festival

Pleebig — mild expletive used by Furlow: I'm not a pleebig ocular physician.

Pneuma — something vital to Delvians: I would risk my pneuma for the chance to go home.

Prabakto — Hynerian term for rascal, as in: Just go, you lucky prabakto.

Pronga — animal whose smoked sinew is easy to prepare

Prowler — two-seater, top-of-the-line Peacekeeper ship similar to a jet fighter

Qualta Blade/Qualta Rifle — Luxan weapon, serving as both a pulse rifle and a twin-bladed weapon powerful enough to cut through stone

Rasklak — hot, strong drink served on Peacekeeper bases (probably alcoholic)

Samat — Acquaran unit of measurement for height, as in: A full samat bigger than Talio or Ku-Mah.

Sevva crystals — an explosive

Shakloom — sea creature found on Acquara, caught for food

Shakloom jerky — another Hynerian delicacy

Shilquen — Luxan musical instrument D'Argo plays to soothe Pilot

Shivvies — Nebari term for male private parts, as in: Don't get your shivvies in an uproar!

Snurching — Nebari slang term for stealing

Solar day — unit of time roughly equivalent to one Earth day

StarBurst — Leviathan leap into hyperspace

Terleum mollusks — more food enjoyed by Hynerians

Terok — Luxan internal organ which D'Argo injures, causing internal bleeding

Tinked — Nebari term for mad: Are you tinked?

Trads — Sebacean unit of power

Translator microbes — microscopic life form able to translate almost any language

Trat — something foul: It smells like trat!

Trinkas bath — form of ablution enjoyed by Hynerians

Tronkan shrill singer — a rather noisy creature: We're broadcasting our position like a two-headed Tronkan shrill singer!

Veen — another Nebari expletive: Oh my veen!

Wakket hole — Sebacean slang for mouth, as in: Shut your wakket hole.

Wanta chant — Delvian chant to assist work efficiency

Watruka plant — deceptively pleasant-looking plant that hides danger

Welnitz — another of Furlow's expletives: You dumb welnitz!

Yenen — species that the garbologist Staanz claims to be to excuse his lack of mivonks

Yotz — Hynerian expletive: What the yotz are you doing?

Yuvok — ointment to help Rygel breathe

Zacrons — unit of measurement: The magnadrift mesh known as the flax is seventy-five million zacrons long.